Mourning

Has

Broken

Printed in the United States of America

First Printing, 2014

ISBN 978-1495397172

Humming Bird Press, LLC

St. Louis, MO 63139

Fax: (509) 275-2544

Hello,

My hope is you find some peace & comfort between these pages. Let yourself rest, grief has no time-clock, no season, no end date.

. May you find some joy in the purity of your sweet sorrow.

Love & blessings,
Rose

Cover Photograph by Denise Beckmann

Cover Photograph Dedication

In Loving Memory of Our Youngest Child,

and Our Only Blessed Son

Connor Samuel Sher.

Sunrise 2-11-1994 ~ Sunset 11-13-2011

FoReVeR 17

Our Angel Boyos has Gone Fishing with The Lord

Parents Harold Sher and Denise Beckmann

Big Sisters Jessica Sher, Amy Sher, and Andrea Sher;

Connor has helped to inspire a special group:

Angel Mom's Over St. Louis

Our family is so very grateful. Many prayers,

((hugs)), and blessings!

Dedication

To My 3 'Lil Angels~ Shannon, Kimberly and Tina,

Always and Forever

My Husband, who supports and loves me through everything, every day and every night~ you are a blessing and a true friend, thank you for your love and support.

My Sons in law, Jason, Michael and Jake~ they couldn't be more wonderful than any sons, God could have given me.

My Grand Eight~ Ana, Jason (J-Bug), Selena, Eva, Mikey, Aubrie, Gus and Olivia (LuLu) These eight kids warm my heart and teach me how to live every day. Their smiles are infectious and their love is pure joy.

My Family and Friends~ who have prayed with me, wept with me, laughed with me and sat by silently when I needed to be alone. They know me and met my needs with grace and all the love one could ever ask for in life. I am grateful beyond words.

And Christine Jaco, a new friend and contributor to this book, and I hope all the rest to come. You are brilliant and warm and loving~ thank you for your selfless time and efforts to bring this book to life.

My Creator~ Thank you for My Life in Jesus Christ, My Savior, who strengthens and unconditionally loves me in this world and the next.

Christine Jaco Bio

Christine is a Master in Business Administration with an emphasis in Human Resource Development at Webster University, St. Louis, Missouri; Bachelor of Liberal Studies at Southern Illinois University Edwardsville and an Associate in Applied Science at Southwestern Illinois College.

Much of Christine's pursuit of knowledge has been influenced by theoretical and philosophical psychology and motivated by a desire to understand human behavior

Christine is devoted to lifelong learning with an emphasis in progressive skills and abilities as

a capable supporter of healing and soul sister of grieving mothers.

Christine resides in Cahokia, Illinois with her youngest daughter.

Michelle Moceri Bio

Michelle Moceri is a certified medium and clairvoyant. She holds a bachelors degree in Metaphysical Science and has a license with the World Wide Ministry of Metaphysics. Michelle is a metaphysical teacher and Reiki Master practitioner in energy healing. She has studied extensively over the past 5 years, including studies in England and has taken master classes with renowned medium John Holland.

Michelle co-facilitates How To Raise Your Vibration workshops across the country with Master teacher and healer Paige Hall-Ferraro, teaching others how to shed density and negativity to receive more light and abundance into their lives.

Michelle resides in Colorado Springs with her husband and three children. To Michelle what she does is not work, but a privilege in assisting others on their healing path, and in channeling messages from the other side

Foreword

This book and those to follow are wonderful examples of how one woman turned her grief around by the grace of God. Prayer and love of family is getting her through the loss of her daughter. Her grief that was once filled with despair is now taking on the life of being of service to others and discovering her new walk with God.

Her daughter Shannon is surrounded my God's pure radiant love with her continued evolving into a brilliant soul. I have done many mediumship readings for people, and over time I can't remember what occurred, but with connecting with Shannon, it made an impact on me. Shannon came through so strong and determined, but I was also so impressed with Rose. The gut wrenching heartache she was feeling, I was feeling too through her energy. Yet, there was resolve in her voice and a determination to help others that have experienced what her and her family has gone through. To me, that is pretty amazing to want to help others while she is still grieving so hard herself. Part of it I feel, did Rose want to have people know who her daughter was and carry on her legacy as a steward of those that needed help and guidance, as she has proven in her charity work.

The connection they have is palpable and maybe even more so since she has crossed over. You see, Rose and Shannon are on a mission so they have to be in sync to accomplish God's work to be of service to others on their healing journey. This isn't a book about religion, but simply her relationship with the Divine and the magical connection with her daughter in the afterlife.

When I talk to Rose about how her writing and grief groups are going, she responds mostly with, "Michelle, I am just amazed how everything is coming together and falling into place." I tell people when they are in alignment with their higher self / higher power then miracles happen. God and the angels hear our prayers and when we are in that alignment to co-create the possibilities are endless. You have heard that saying "It takes a village." Well that is what is happening in heaven and here on earth. The hoops spirit jumps through to make things happen for us in that exact moment is amazing. Many times its doors closing or relationships ending to get us back on the right path to fulfill our destiny. That is why it is so important to keep going, keep asking questions, keep determined, keep healing, keep loving,   and to keep your heart open to God and the possibilities. Moving energy is growing energy and expansion of the mind and soul.

   I hope you find comfort in this book. It's an outpouring of Rose's honesty, heartache and strength to find healing in the most tragic of circumstances. If you are going through a loss of some kind, please take solace in knowing you're never alone and there is no right or wrong to the grieving process. Rose's story is inspirational and will help many heal with prayer and conviction. I am honored to have known Rose and look forward to her continued growth in how a mother grieves through prayer and forgiveness.

   Michelle Moceri

Preface

Almost a whole year has gone by Shanny. I feel like I have grown up a lot this past year. I miss you so much but I can work with my sadness and channel it better now. My energy has some direction and I can, for the most part, pray my way through the really rough spots. I have decided to share my thoughts and feelings with others who are in pain. I want to help. I tried to figure out a lot of stuff by myself and it was so hard. Maybe, there are others who wish they had someone to communicate with or just to listen to them share or vent.

Some days, I just want to talk and I want to know, others, sadly-sometimes feel the same way I do, because it means I am not crazy. It kind of validates what I am going through because it can feel surreal at times.

I don't know, this has been a very difficult year, but it has also been very rewarding. I am stronger than I ever thought I could be. I am loved more than I ever imagined, and I am truly blessed in a way that I can't even explain.

What I do know is this: The power of prayer and faith is mighty. God listens and He answers, not always according to our requests, but always according to what is best for us. I am learning and I am growing-now, I am in a place to finally give. Thank you, Jesus!

I don't have any fancy titles, degrees or letters after my name. I am a mother who lost her daughter on February 10, 2011. I am grieving and taking my journey through grief. That qualifies me as expert on this subject.

Lately, I am feeling like an expert on the subject of grief-the pain, excruciating, blinding at times, makes me want to cry, vomit, scream, moan, talk, laugh hysterically and shut my eyes and remember her detail by detail. Most of all, I have learned to Pray-constantly. Sometimes, it is only one word, but God gets it. He cries with me sometimes. I know it, because I feel His warm and ever so gentle essence in the midst of my cold and lonely world when I want nothing more than to touch her or kiss her again.

You might be asking me, how old was your daughter? Young! My daughter was 34 years young, an adult to most-but always my baby. You see, it doesn't matter how old or young our children are when they are taken back to Heaven, I don't think we are ever ready to give them back.

Please, take a moment to hug your babies if they are close enough-or tell them with a verbal 'hug' if they aren't, just how much they mean to you-not generically either-oh, honey-you mean the world to me....why? Tell-them-why! Is it because they make you laugh? Is it because they brought you lunch when you weren't expecting it? Is it because they are always thinking of you and calling you out of the blue? It doesn't matter why-but it will matter to them-that you share it with them-I promise. Tell them, don't wait. We'll talk again soon. Please share your ideas and thoughts with me. There are so many bumps in this road-this journey takes a lot of twists and turns, I need all the friends along the way I can find.

Sunday, February 5, 2012

Going Back...Last Year at This Time

This week will be very difficult for me. I seem to be remembering the events from last year at this time day by day. I caught myself pulling out a calendar and checking my notes on it. As I read the captions, Jewelry Party, Fundraiser, Children's Liturgy, etc. I ask myself: Why? Do I want to punish myself? Do I want to somehow close my eyes and go back in time? Of course! Wouldn't you?

Last year at this time I had Shanny and I would call her and talk with her, and see her and touch her and ignore her calls, if I chose to. And now, reality is...I can't do any of those things. I must tell you–it kind of bugs me when people say, "she is here in spirit." I know that, but really? It just isn't the same as kissing her on the forehead and smelling the sweet scent of just showered skin and freshly washed hair. I got to do that sometimes, if I was at the house and she would grab a shower while I was there. I miss that.

She would come downstairs in her PJ bottoms and T-shirt, hair in a towel and snuggle with her blanket on the couch. For a time, we would forget how old she was, and I might sneak in a cuddle, she liked her head and back rubbed sometimes. Especially, if she wasn't feeling well and I would go over just to be with her. I don't know that I made a practice of doing it, but I did it a few times. You see, it isn't how much I did something; it is that I did it and I can remember it. I am thankful for that gift. God is good. I lean heavily on prayer throughout my day. When I get up in the morning, I still try to forget she is really gone. When the reality hits me, I pray. As I get ready for work I pray for focus at my job and patience throughout the day. On my way to work I thank God for the day, and the day before-just in case I forgot the night before, I want to be covered. Even though, I know Him well, and He gets me. Depending on my day, I share many "Aha" moments with Him as my cubicle is filled with pictures of my family and grand kids. I have many opportunities to share with people throughout the day and when I meet new 'friends', as well. I end my work

correspondence with–Have a Blessed Day.

I believe in sharing, sprinkling seeds of faith everywhere

and letting them grow and blossom. Today, the pain is not

physical. I am going to smile and relax with the knowledge that this

gloomy day has a purpose–I am here, where I need to be right now.

Tomorrow, is another day and I will pray for direction as I

continue my journey through grief, knowing I am not alone–My

Friend, My Father is with me.

He is giving me the strength and courage to make this journey. The Power of Prayer and Faith make it possible for me to grow and share along the way.

Tuesday, February 7, 2012

Monday, Monday...

Do you remember that song? Life was so simple-but there

is joy amidst the grief. For me, it often comes in the form of my

grandchildren. Over the weekend, it was a birthday party for my

grandson, Mikey. He gives great hugs and has the sweetest of

wishes...will you play with me? How can you not smile and find the

inner peace in that simple and loving request?

I am blessed with Eight such wonderful little people in my

life. They all have their own personalities that I dearly love.

I am beginning to get to know each one through finding out

what it is they enjoy. Because it isn't all about me! Last night I got

a great phone call. My granddaughter Evie wanted MeeMaw to

come over. What a treat. A year ago I would probably have said I

was too tired, too frustrated from work, too full of myself...but

God is teaching me, this journey isn't just about me. If I open my

eyes and close my mouth (He whispers in a loving way) you will find some joy in the midst of your grief, I promise. He has never let me down so far.

So, after our own version of American Idol, stowing away on a Pirate Ship, taking refuge in a Giant Castle and playing hide-n-seek, I felt sufficiently loved for one evening. I am able to accept that some days kids aren't in a giving mood. They might be in a "needy" place. As grown-ups, we really aren't much different. So, at the end of the night if they don't jump in my arms and exclaim that I am the best MeeMaw in the whole wide world–it's okay. They just gave me more than they could ever know–they gave me a glimpse of their world, and that is priceless.

What I am learning on this journey is that sometimes pain is necessary. Sometimes, we create our own pain, and sometimes we grow out of the pain. God will never give us more than we can handle–pain, grief or sadness; we just need to reach beyond ourselves for joy. Reach out and put your arms around a child–that's joy!

As this week draws closer to the 10th, I feel myself begin to withdraw a little. I am hurting. I miss my child, my baby. But I will not close out the moments of joy that each day can bring and I can share. I ask God for strength and courage and only the wisdom I need to do His will. Soon, I will begin my journey through the last year and how I got to "now." Writing is such a pressure release. It physically helps relieve the pain of the grief. Sharing is so wonderful-even if no one reads it-the written word-heals.

Thursday, February 9, 2012

The Day It All Began

It's so hard to believe-a year has gone by and I remember it like it was yesterday. Jas called about 2:30 in the afternoon from the ER. Shannon is having some problems and they want to run some tests, she'd really like it if you came up to be with her...and I left work, went home, grabbed a few things and went straight to the hospital, knowing I wouldn't be home again that night. If Shanny had to spend the night, so did I.

It didn't matter that she was 34 years old. It didn't matter that I was married and had to work the next day. It didn't matter, that people would think I was overreacting. She was scared and I was staying. That's all that mattered.

Shanny was scheduled for a stress test the next morning; it was more for precaution said one nurse. It was due to a bad EKG said another nurse. But before morning we had to get through the night. Jas stayed and then went and picked up the kids and brought them up to visit with mom. I kept a low profile,

reading while they visited, praying, worrying and trying to look like

all was...good.

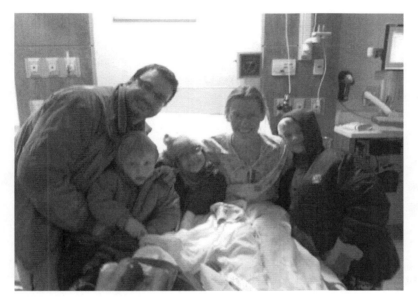

When visiting hours were over, Jas slowly said his good-

byes and the kids gave their hugs and kisses and off they went

promising to talk in the morning, and 3 little tired beings and 1

grown one made their way out of the room and down the hall to the

elevator.

Shannon and I were quiet at first, and then little by little we

danced with the elephant in the room. I scooted my chair closer to

her bed and took her hand. "I love you. I am so proud of you. I know you are scared, but you are doing this anyway, because you love Jas and the kids so much, you're doing it to make sure you are really all right. I 'm proud you are facing your fear." "Mom, I am scared. Something just doesn't feel right." "I know, and that's why this is so important." I took her hand in mine and gently kissed her fingertips and then I stroked her silky hair and kissed her forehead. God will be with you, I said.

She got up and puttered around the room a bit, talked on the phone, worked on her laptop, read for a while, and wrote love notes to her hubby and kids. That was Shanny, though...always thinking of what others were feeling. In this case, what affect her being in the hospital was having on the kids and Jas. Through her fear, she prayed her rosary and tossed and turned.

We spoke in spurts through the night-little words of love, 'do you need anything?' 'Mom, are you still here?' ' Hold my hand'...'I'm right here, sweetie'...Even though I honestly thought she was going to be fine and come home with us in a day or two, I didn't like seeing her frightened and so vulnerable. My head was telling me I was being over protective and probably over reacting to the situation, but my heart was telling me I was right where I needed to be.

Soon, I could hear her breathing and I closed my eyes and slept until I heard the nurse in the morning, and Shanny was moving about the room. Another day to hurry up and wait, another day to worry, give it to God, wrestle it back, and pray for patience because no one was in a hurry to find any answers.

A stress test is a reasonably simple test for a healthy young 34 year old woman. Except Shanny had questions and the doctor had a short supply of patience and understanding? What about me? I had a case of the "Mother needs a word with the doctor."

Shanny looked so upset after her stress tests it nearly broke my heart. There she was in a wheelchair in the hall... "I think I made him really mad at me." I knew this wasn't going to be simple...

Friday, February 10, 2012

365 Days do not Make It Hurt Less – But It Does Hurt Less Often

Now there are times when the memories don't cause me to gasp and clutch something or someone too hard. I can smile when I see her face in a photograph. I can speak her name out loud and not have my stomach tie in knots because I ache to hug her again. I have those days, too. The horrible ones-tears are the only thing I taste that day. I don't answer my phone because I really don't care what you have to say right now, it just doesn't matter. Sleep is either never ending or I can't remember when I last slept longer than 20 minutes in a stretch. Sadness takes my breath away and there is no energy to remember to let the dog out or back in or feed the cat or I...it's just one of those days. Yes, I still have them, not 7 in a row, not even once a week sometimes... Now I have respite from the devastating heartache of constant pain. I know

God has blessed me. He has touched my heart and warmed my spirit again.

I can wake up and not dread the morning or fear the darkness at night. When the clock shows 8:10 pm, I can take a breath and live through it. When a Thursday comes, I do not close my eyes and force myself to sleep until dusk. This is how 365 days have changed me. But it is not just the passing of time that has brought about change. I was awakened in the Spirit and my faith has grown. I have questioned God's purpose in taking my daughter. I have ranted and raved and pounded my fist. I have cried until I could not cry any more tears. And I have shut my eyes and tried to sleep through the nightmares.

Then I prayed.

Then I asked God to help me.

Then I thanked God for loving me.

Then I cried and God held me.

Then we prayed.

God, I said-I don't understand.

I know-He said.

I miss my baby, Lord. I am so saddened

and lost. I am afraid

I might not be strong enough to do this alone.

You are not alone.

I feel alone. I feel sad. I feel angry. I feel confused. I feel

sick, Lord. Help me, please.

You are not alone.

Then I cried and God held me.

Then I prayed.

Then I asked God to help me.

Then I thanked God for loving me.

Then I cried and God held me.

Then we talked.

God, I still don't understand.

I know.

I don't think I have to understand.

I know.

I still miss my baby and love her. I will never forget her.

Even if I choose to live again and work and find some joy in life I

will never forget her.

I know.

God, I am on a journey of love

-healing love.

I know.

And so it is...365 days and counting.

Words are Powerful

The doctor had chastised Shanny for her fear of the dye and drug they put in the stress test to measure your heart rate and your reaction. I am not medically inclined at all, so I have no idea what they wanted to do or use but I do know my daughter. She was scared for a reason.

After Shanny got settled down in her room, she said, "Mom, I just don't want them to use that drug, (she knew the name) it makes my heart race and I don't need it. I asked the doctor about the dye and he got really ugly with me. I just need time to digest it all mom, I have to understand it a little better." That made sense to me, so I went in search of someone to explain it to her.

Thankfully, a wonderful nurse was on duty and she came in later with a computer printout and notes and went through the procedure with Shannon so she could understand everything and it quieted her anxiety. I can't help thinking if that doctor had taken just a moment to think about what she was feeling, instead of being in such a hurry, she would have been more emotionally prepared for that stress test. Shannon agreed to the stress test with the dye and I thought we were in for a peaceful night.

Jas and the kids came up to visit, and I stayed until visiting hours were over for the night. As I got ready to go, Shanny asked-Mom, are you leaving? I said, yes-I needed to get home and showered and I'd go into work in the morning and then come in when she knew about what time she was to have her test. I could see the disappointment, but I really felt she was going to be okay through the night. Jas and the kids stayed a while and we managed to sneak in ice cream for everyone and lots of hugs. Eventually, I did leave about 9:30 that evening after Jas and the kids, and Shanny although not happy promised to call me in the morning so I knew what time to come up.

On the way home, I cried and prayed at the same time. Please let her be ok. She looks just fine, Lord. Please just let this be a test and nothing more. For so long, Shanny had wanted me to spend more time with her. I was always too busy, with work, new marriage, new job, and jewelry business. But I did manage to do

Children's Liturgy with her and we really enjoyed that together. We bonded over my jewelry business.

She encouraged me to do things I wanted to do but wasn't sure I could. When I look back, her simple request was for my time, my love, something I should have given much more freely than I did. But in life, there are no do-overs when you lose a loved one.

There are do-betters. I am learning how to set my priorities according to God's will and not my own. That is helping me every day on my journey. I had to learn to be quiet and listen, and for folks who know me...that can be a challenge, am I right?

Sunday, February 12, 2012

When "I'll See You In an Hour"

Never Happens.

After a long restless night, filled with worry and doubt-I slept. I went home from the hospital late thinking Shanny looked fine, although anxious. I felt I needed to get sleep in a bed and not a rolling pleather chair that stayed cold and the blankets smelled of antiseptic. Besides, I decided work had to be a priority for now, unless issues changed and things took a different turn. For now, all was good with the world. I got up early and called Shannon, guilt for leaving the hospital set in and I thought if she really felt I needed to be with her, I'd go back up...work could wait another day.

Shanny told me to go on to work, the doctors hadn't been in, actually no one had been in yet and it was already after 7:00 am. Whatever happened to shift changes and nurses popping in to check on you and doctors making rounds, and the patient never getting sleep because there were always medical people in the room asking questions or adjusting something or administering meds? I guess if Shannon had been on any machines or i.v.'s, we would have seen someone. Honestly, I had to hunt someone down most of the time to ask a question or get an answer. This day wasn't starting out any differently.

Jas got to the hospital after he dropped off the kids to school and Gus to pre-school. I called back and there was still no news about 9:00 am. Jas went on a hunt of his own-a hunt for some answers.

My phone rang about 10:45 and it was Jas. They scheduled Shan for a cardiac cath at 2:00 pm. WHAT?!? WHY!?! I'm not sure but that is the plan. OK-I'll leave at lunch time unless you think I need to get there earlier. No, that should be fine-if anything changes-I'll call you back.

At 11:15 my supervisor said "Rose, when are you leaving?" In a minute, I said. Just let me finish this last whatever it was that was so important. I walked out of there at 11:30 or so and by the time I got to my car, I was in a panic. I don't know why, probably guilt. Guilt for not staying the night before, guilt for not asking

enough questions, guilt for not being a good enough mom, guilt for

not leaving work earlier and what if I don't get there on time and

they take her early and my phone is dead and Jas tried to call but

couldn't reach me.... I walked in her room at 12:10 and she was on

her laptop and looked up and smiled. Hi, mom...

(Breathe)-Hi, Shanny-bug...

And we waited. We talked, I held her hand, she whispered

she was scared, I told her how proud of her I was that she was

doing this. I rubbed her forehead, it usually soothed her, and

today I was trying to soothe myself. The longer it was taking, the

more anxious I became. I know very little about medical

procedures. But I knew this was way more invasive than a stress

test with dye. I knew of people who had them and said it was

routine now; nothing to worry about, stop being over dramatic.

She wrote in her journal, she wrote notes, she prayed, she spoke

on the phone, she smiled, and then about 2:10 a nurse came in and

said there had been an emergency and the cath lab had called,

Shan's cath would be pushed back. It would be done today, but she didn't know what time. And so, we waited. About 2:30 Shannon said...I'm so hungry, maybe I should just wait until tomorrow for this test, I haven't eaten since yesterday. What if the doctors are too tired to do it now? Really, I think I should just wait. Oh fear or premonition or the knowledge of what was to come?

Jas finally spoke and said I'm not sure if that's an option, honey. Let's give it a little time and if they don't call for you soon, we'll see what we can do about getting you something to eat. And so, we waited. You could feel the tension in the air. Oh the frustration of dragging this whole calamity out. No communication, no real plan or direction, no answers to questions, nothing but a ticking clock. At 3:15 a gurney was rolled into the room and Shannon was moving from the bed to the gurney and all of a sudden, we were in the hall exchanging kisses and hugs and I ran back for one more. I made the sign of the cross on her forehead and said God bless you, God be with you. I love you and I'll see you in an hour. She said," Love you, too, Mom."

That hour turned into 5 hours of hell. I never got to feel her beating heart again. Her hug was just a memory now and I will always think of her last words to me as my final gift. "Love you, Mom..."

My baby would not wake up and kiss her husband and hug her babies. This is truly what she lived for-her family. She wouldn't attend the Justice for All Ball in 2 weeks and wear the new sash she just bought for her dress. She wouldn't see J-Bug take 4th in the Pinewood Derby, or Gus have his party at the pizza parlor, or Evie sell over 200 boxes of GS cookies. She wouldn't fuss at her sisters about how to raise their kids, or annoy them with her phone calls, or tease me about waxing my moustache or making sure I was flossing enough...

God, what I wouldn't give for just one more day...but that wouldn't be enough either. The truth is, I would never be ready to give my babies back. Even though I know they are only on 'loan' from God. They are mine while they are here and that won't ever be long enough. I took so much for granted, right up until the end. I believed with all my heart I would see her in an hour...and that hour never came.

Now, I am learning to say "I love you" more often... To listen more closely... To make memories while we have the opportunity...

I am only sorry it took losing a daughter to teach me such simple life lessons-lessons she tried to teach me while she was here...when I was too often too busy or too tired. Shannon knew the true gifts this life had to offer were born of our faith and our family. She lived her life in pursuit of both.

She left this world a better place for having been in it-she wrapped her arms around life and gave it one giant hug! She left this world having been loved by so many...including a mother who leaned over a bassinet 34 years ago and whispered, "I love you, sweetie," just like I did today...only today she whispered back

"Love you, too, Mom."

Wednesday, February 15, 2012

Feb. 14 Will Never Be the Same

For many this day represents hearts and candy and cards and cupid. Don't get me wrong, it did for me too, until last year. Then, after I had all the grandkids Valentines set aside, all the stuffed animals tagged, and all the cards addressed. This day took on a whole new meaning for me.

I buried my daughter on this day. Time doesn't stop for any of us, I know that. And no one would have thought this day we know for love and flowers and candy, would be so different in a year. The stuffed animals sat on the table, the valentines were never mailed. The candy was never delivered and the grandkids gifts sat unwrapped and undelivered for almost a year before I could move them and pack them away.

No, this day will never be the same. I hope and pray for peace and serenity so I can better face it next year. Not for my sake, but the grandkids-they deserve better. Their world should not be overshadowed with sadness and heartbreak. Their world should not be broken and empty-their world should be filled with candy hearts and balloons and valentine boxes and all the things kids have in their world, including a mother, a wife for daddy, a daughter, a sister, an aunt...

My husband, thoughtful as he is brought home a plant for the yard-a hyacinth bulb, a card and a sweet let's go out to dinner note. That is all I could handle. He gets me, I know he is sensitive to my feelings and would do more, but honestly, I don't want or need more.

I want to be in a better place for the girls and the grand kids. I am just not quite there yet. I am doing the best I can today. Kim and Tina both called to see how I was doing. We all know what we are thinking; we just don't want to say it out loud. We miss you, Shanny. Today and every day, this day really is about love, our love for each other and you.

Jas posted beautiful pictures on Facebook. His strength amazes me. I love and respect him so much. He loved my Shannon in a beautiful way. Their love was rare. They fought for their love, and built the strongest of loves. It was not easy. It is not my story to share. But I will tell you, their love is a true love story.

And so another day has passed-maybe next year will be different-maybe I will be able to deliver candy and stuffed animals to the grandkids again. Maybe, I will recognize the love in my heart wasn't put there to stay. Love isn't love until we give it away. I did not utter the words all day, because they hurt too much, but I feel safer here...Happy Valentine's Day, Shanny

I love you.

I love you.

I love you.

xoxoxo

Mom

Thursday, February 16, 2012

The Face of a Mother's Grief

I saw you at the store today and you nodded in my direction and hurriedly moved on. It is the same at church on Sunday sometimes. The silence can be awkward. When I see you on the street or at the kids' games or the park...you don't know what to say or what to ask. I will tell you the truth if you ask me.

So, be prepared for the answer. And if you really don't want to know, please do not ask - it takes a lot of energy some days to converse. You see, the passing of a year is not a magic number and the hurt does not stop or go away. A mother does not forget even the slightest of details about her child. A mother will always remember. It doesn't matter if you have only had your child a day, a week, a month or years-you know your child like no one else-every inch of them from head to toe. And so, is a mother's love. From the moment we feel them move inside. We become "mother". We love, we protect, we feel and grieve as a mother for our child, no matter how long we have known or loved them. No matter if they have grown up and moved out of our homes married and have children of their own-they are and will forever be ours.

That's my question today. How do you recognize the face of a grieving mother? Will her face be forever changed by the tears she has shed? Will her smile lines, become grief wrinkles? Do the dark circles under her eyes ever go away? What do you suppose she is thinking, if by chance you glimpse even a brief moment of something other than sorrow? Will you recognize joy should you see it on her face?

I remember the first time I smiled after Shanny passed away. I felt like a criminal. How dare I feel anything even remotely close to "happy?" This was after weeks of moving as if I were in a constant state of numbness. I was unaware of anything or anyone around me and slept about 18 to 20 hours a day for the first 3 weeks. And then there were nights when sleep would not come at all. Those nights were spent lying awake replaying the last few days of Shannon's life over and over again.

And then, something beautiful began to happen and the Power of Prayer began to shape the face of this grieving mother. I began to notice I wasn't feeling numb all the time. I could breathe and feel if I allowed myself the freedom to do so. I wasn't as fragile as I thought I was, and I am as strong as I ask God to be. I can face this grief-a mother's grief...if I turn to God for help. And so, I did.

I wept, I prayed, I begged for answers, and I praised God for loving me even though I questioned His knowledge and His wisdom. I believe in Heaven. I believe in life after death and salvation and the whole nine yards. I am a happy believer who may not understand God's will, but I know that God loves me and has His arms wrapped lovingly around my daughter-His child, who He loaned me for 34 years to love in this world.

I know she is happy beyond my understanding and comprehension. I also hurt for her husband and children who are here, missing their mommy and wife.

This creates quite a struggle for me. I love my baby and I miss her, and yet, I know she is in a far better place-where I hope to be some day. And then, I think of her husband, Jas and his sorrow and the sadness and pain her children go through, and I ask myself. How can you ever feel joyful again? So what, that you hear the song of a bird on a wintry day? So what, that the sun shines on the snow and warms the winter air? So what, that God has given you another day to live and breathe and share your love with your family...so what?

And I pray...please, Lord, let me turn my face to you, always to you -this face of a mother's grief. Amen.

Friday, February 17, 2012

Prayer is Powerful; Faith is a Gift, and God Is the Best Listener

I am blessed today, as always to have a choice. I can choose to see the beauty in this day-the treasures that it holds; or I can choose to get stuck in the sadness and pain of my grief. If I choose to see the beauty, it doesn't mean I am forgetting, it simply means that at this moment I am choosing to experience God's blessing. How do I go from grieving to experiencing the beauty the day holds?

For me, the answer is Prayer... Prayer is a word that for many is taboo. It reeks of religious context, formality, conformity; some even associate it with a cult. Prayer for me is simply a conversation with God.

I know prayers that I love to recite—the Our Father, because someone very special to me taught me a very valuable lesson about that prayer. Sometimes we get so caught up in reciting it, we don't really feel the words. How sincere could it be for me if I wasn't really aware of what I was saying?

I learned that prayer is about so much more than remembered words from my childhood, it is about love and forgiveness, and truly getting to know and love our Lord on a personal level, so much so that I trusted Him enough to know His will should be done-not mine, because He is the ultimate in Love and Understanding. He Is. Once, I grasped that, I felt a stirring very deep in my core and I knew all would be as it should once I let go...

Years of trying to take control back and wrestle with my faith left me wandering from church to church and faith to faith...My Friend, Jesus-He never left my side, I chose to run away from what I knew was right because along with it comes responsibility. Doing what is right is never easy, no matter how old or young you are or what stage of your faith walk you are in...I am drifting off subject here, but I get so excited about sharing about the Power of Prayer and how Great He Is...even in the deepest, darkest days of my grief, when I miss my daughter so much I can't breathe, He comforts me.

Prayer I believe is universal...we may not all pray the same words, to the one I call God, you may call Him-Higher Power, or He may be a She, or you may not be a believer at this time.

But I will tell you one thing I know for sure...My God listens. He hears the prayers of all people, in every language, in every church, in every country. Everywhere...He listens to our hearts, He knows them, each one of us, individually, by name...He created us...to love and be loved. When I lost my daughter, I cannot tell you the pain or the depth of that pain, I went into shock. My family went into prayer and requested prayers from co-workers, friends, church members...we are not all of the same faith in my family, but God doesn't have a preferred list, He has open arms and ears...

Weeks went by and I was wrapped in a protective cocoon of sorts. I didn't feel much of anything and existed, more than lived-by the grace of God. I only knew short, simple messages were all I could offer God then.

Please God, help me. I don't know if I have the strength to come back from this, Lord...there is so much I should have done and wanted to do and Lord, I can't ever kiss her again...I can't describe the pain, I can only say, my comfort came moment by moment, and then hour by hour and sometimes a few hours at a time would go by and I would be thinking of something she had said or I said.

And the waves of grief and pain would wash over me again and again until I was exhausted from the knowledge that it wasn't going to change. My baby was now in the hands of her Heavenly Father. I must say, I left most of the praying to other folks, I just didn't have the energy, the overwhelming sadness and loss was threatening to rob me of my relationship with My Father. Not because I was angry, not yet anyway. I was tired, too tired to pray, too tired to reach out. Too tired to turn to Him for strength and comfort and too tired to turn away. But others were praying, all over the place, people I didn't know, people who felt a kinship because they too had children, people who knew how close I was to my girls, people who could only imagine the devastation, but also knew the power of prayer.

Then, one day in the routine of my waking, being somewhat disoriented, realizing why I was just waking up...feeling truth slowly creep into my brain and my heart, I began to weep, let me tell it like it really was...I was bawling my eyes out, sobbing, hiccoughing, begging God to let me wake up from the nightmare and finally exhausting my-self and hoping sleep would come again. Instead what I felt was a slow steady tingle from my toes to the very top of my head. I remember thinking I was having a heart attack and I started to ask God for forgiveness for all my many sins and failures. I was asking if this was really my time...please let my daughter be there to greet me. I remember feeling scared a little, but more excited than frightened. And then, when I really became aware of my surroundings again, I was still on the bed, laying on my back, and wondering what had happened. There was no pain, no headache, and no dizziness. Just an overwhelming sense of peace and serenity...

I felt as if I was beginning to understand this journey. It isn't God's choosing, to make it painful for us when we lose a loved one. God created a perfect world. We, us–all of us are imperfect and make mistakes, bad choices, errors in judgment. But in that instant I knew the question would never be–Why did God let this happen? I knew if I felt anger, it would be okay, God, my loving Father, gets me. He is saddened by what goes on in this world, and He grieves with me because He does understand. You see– He lost His Son and so He knows the grief I struggle with daily.

Even on my loneliest day–I am not alone. On the day the most devastating news was delivered to me, I was not alone. And I am not on this journey alone. So, even in my simplest prayer–I know God hears me... He knows my heart and He listens with His...

And so my prayer: Dear God, thank you for this day, for my family, my friends and the friends I have yet to meet. Let the gift of Your love be seen through me and shared through Your words. Help us all love one another, as You love us, forgive one another, as You forgive us, and believe in what we cannot see, or feel, or hear. Help us know that we should treasure each day You give us in this life, believing eternity is real. Help us reach beyond ourselves knowing You are there to hear this, and every prayer we speak with our lips or with our hearts.

Prayer... A simple, beautiful language that really is universal...

Sunday, February 19, 2012

Two Words...

This month my Shanny was gone a year as of February 10th. It's amazing how fast the months went by and at the same time how slowly time crept along. Sometimes, I would will it to be pre-Feb.10, 2011 in my mind when life was described by most as "normal". Whatever that is. For me it was working, spending time with my husband, working on the Jewelry business and catching up with the kids and grandkids when time allowed. Now, that thought makes me ill. When time allowed, I dictated when time allowed. I chose to be too busy or too tired or too wrapped up in this or that. I am frustrated with myself for taking so much for granted. Who knows what is in store for us? That is why living each day is so very important to me now. I feel robbed some days of time. Time with Shanny.

Watching her with her husband and kids, the loves of her life: shopping and running errands and just being silly when we chose to, and because we could. Seeing her with her sisters and remembering when they were all young. Little wisps of girls, Shanny all blond and so pretty people would stop me and comment on her in the stroller.

Then, Kimmy my little tomboy, rough and tough until she was in her teens and then her softer side emerged. And Tina, my wild child, she is so much like I was when I was young it scares me seeing all of them together-priceless. The memories that get stirred up take me back to a time when being a single mom and working two and three jobs was the norm to keep up with the bills and the rent and expenses of raising three girls.

I remember the struggles of dance school, gymnastics, scouts and flute lessons, one week maybe another instrument the next. We managed though, garage sales and thrift stores -I was way ahead of the times. My saying was-well, it's new to us! I had the love and support of a great family and the Lord; I just didn't always know where the blessings came from or remember to thank those who anonymously donated to my cause.

God had a watchful hand on my life even when I wasn't aware of His presence. He surrounded me always with the Holy Spirit and kept me safe and for the most part, sane.

Even though those times were not always easy they hold some of the most precious memories I would cherish. Maybe it was the struggle, or the closeness of my girls. They were and always will be My Three Little Angels. Their innocence and gentleness of spirit would be a constant reminder of how God had blessed me.

Teenage years brought rebellion and tempers and fits of rage and anger. And yet, the sun continued to shine and the birds would sing. Not every day, but enough to remind me that I was blessed. As the months slipped into years, each daughter took on a personality and spirit of her own. Each one grew into a beautiful woman, mother and wife, and they continued to be close knit sisters, in spite of their differences in child rearing, home decorating and a multitude of issues I would hear about from one or two of the three almost daily. I loved every moment of it. I was always happiest when I had all three with me at the same time.

Sometimes we would dissolve into a fit of laughter over absolutely nothing.

And then again, sometimes they would gang up on me about something I was wearing or my hair or nothing at all. We knew how to love strongly. We loved deeply. We didn't always agree with one another, but we always made up. We knew we would always be there for each other-like the four musketeers reunited...

And so, as I reflect not only on this past year but on many years of my life, I like to hold dearly the childhood hugs and kisses, the school dance dress shopping, those late night phone calls and the whispered-"I know I'm your favorite, mom..." Those are memories forever tucked away that I can look back on and say the two most important words a grieving mother can hear...

Two words that will touch a wounded heart, and remind us how blessed we truly are. Two words that bring great comfort to a grieving mother over time; Two words that reassure a mother that her child has left a mark on the world and made it a better place by having been in it, if only for a little while. Two words when spoken out loud mean so much, like music to the ear when we are sorely missing our babies.

Knowing someone cares is wonderful-that they took the time to express their feelings is awesome and it makes a world of difference to a grieving mother, so please take a moment and share your thoughts with a friend or family member or someone you know is struggling with a loss. After all, it is just two little words.

'I remember'.

LOL...

Today is Presidents' Day. It is a noted holiday for a lot of luckies. That's another one; I just made it up...lot of luckies (LOL)! I am not very texting savvy, so the lingo escaped me. Truly, I didn't know what LOL meant. I honestly thought it meant -lots of love (LOL).

The first time I saw it on a text I thought how sweet it was that my daughter would be so thoughtful and send me her love in a text. She laughed out loud (LOL) when she heard that one!

But in the midst of my grief, I find respite in the moments of pure joy God sends me. One of my favorite pictures of Christ is Him with His head back and laughing. It makes me feel His closeness and the joy He has for each one of us. He knows my delights in the birds and the animals He has graced our world with. When a beautiful red Cardinal sits perched outside my window stark against the winter sky I feel like God placed him there just for me that day at that moment to lighten my heart.

When the man I wave to every morning on the way to work, searches me out and waves first-I know that good morning gesture is just for me, another gift in my day. It feels good to see him smile and look my way, it just feels good!

When our dog, all 95 loving pounds of her, rests her head in my lap or looks in my eyes with her sweet innocent face-that's love.

When one of my grandkids hugs me and says, "I love you Grandma." "Will you come over and spend the night soon?" That is one of the greatest gifts I'll ever receive.

Sometimes, out of nowhere, David just brings home a surprise from the store. Whether it's my favorite candy or a little bouquet of flowers or a new flavor of yogurt...it doesn't matter. I know he was thinking of me, and that makes my heart happy.

I printed out an email from Shanny and keep it on my wall at work. It reads "Love you, Mom." That email brings comfort on some days when I just need to hear her voice or feel her closeness.

You can have your lol meanings, I like mine. I made up another one. What about: lover of life that was my Shanny-a lover of life. She saw the good in everyone and everything. Her cup was always half full, because she would be sharing it daily. She would reach beyond herself and say, that exercise was good. What's next? She knew the importance of making the most of each day. She is my sunshine on a cloudy day...

We all need to know that laughter is okay in the midst of our grief. God sends us all moments of lol (lots of love)...to take on our journey.

How about you? What are your 'lol' moments that get you through the day? Have you made up your own meaning for 'lol?' Share it, please...

You have no idea how much it means to have people share their thoughts, ideas, and prayers at this time. This journey, necessary as it is, can be filled with such deep saddening pain on any given day that the comments you might take a moment to leave on a page, could be what breaks that cycle of grief-if only for a moment or two. So, if you are wondering "would it really matter if I left a comment?" The answer is YES! It matters. It's like sharing a conversation with a friend or getting a much needed hug. It's just a 'Google' away. Really, there's a drop down box when you post a comment-select Google. I don't understand it either, I thought you just typed a message and left it but apparently, you have to choose HOW to leave it? According to my daughter-Mom, just choose Google, lol!!

Thursday, February 23, 2012

Heavenly Nudges

I'm pretty sure we all have them. I remember hearing my mom and aunts when I was a little girl talking about loved ones who had passed on, watching over us. Then, when I got older I remember things like my sisters driving around looking for a parking place and all of a sudden one would appear out of nowhere for them...that's a heavenly nudge. Having someone we love watch over us gives us comfort, and if they help us out a little during the day, that's an added smile!

I know since Shanny has passed many times I have looked upward and said thank you. Usually, it is pertaining to the computer at the time. Shanny and I had a special connection when it came to the computer. She got it-I didn't. She found that rather humorous. That is why this is such a great experience for me. I couldn't have told you what the 'apple' was for on a computer much less how or what a 'blog' was going to do for me. Talk about your Heavenly Nudges...

I can tell you about a few times that I have been in search of something and for the longest time could not find it and all of a sudden-there it was. Recently, I was shopping with Tina for a new pair of pants for her. She had to go on an interview and I wanted her to feel really good and comfortable. We had been shopping for at least 45 minutes, scouring the racks over and over. She found a pair and tried them on and decided she needed a different size. Back to the racks we went in search of that pair of pants. After another 30 minutes, and about fifteen racks later I decided I would check one last place. There they were, the only pair of pants in the whole store that Tina actually felt just right wearing, in her size in the wrong place, at the right time! That is a Heavenly Nudge.

I remember shopping for my wedding dress when Shanny was here. My girls and I ran everywhere looking for just the right dress. We had a lot of laughs, at my expense as they had me try on some really hideous dresses but it was so much fun. Shannon had dresses draped across her shoulders around her neck and over her arms.

Tina took a different approach to shopping by actually searching the racks for a suitable dress, but we really had a fun day. The kicker was the dress I ended up with was one of the dresses Shanny found on a clearance rack! We all had a good laugh.

Usually, I am running crazy looking for my clothes for work in the morning. I have tried to put an outfit together the night before and sometimes that works, but on occasion, I'll wake up and it just doesn't bode well that morning. I will have a pair of pants in one hand and go in search of a particular top-closet, drawers, extra bedroom closet, downstairs wash area.

I'm fixated on this one top, of course, by now, I've seen dozens of other tops that would be fine, but I want the one that I have in mind that I cannot find...I give up. I have another cup of coffee and try again. Then, I look in the exact same place I looked the first time-and there it is-right in front of my eyes-as if it had been found and put there. A Heavenly Nudge, I like to think so.

I can't tell you how many times I have put my tax information or a bill in one place and discovered it wasn't where I know I put it but after hours of searching the house from top to bottom, I will find it in a very conspicuous place, (I could almost hear a giggle) because I did this a lot when the girls were young. They teased me about getting "old-timers" because I was so forgetful.

Have you had many experiences like this? When you can almost feel a loved one watching over you? Guiding you? It is such a comforting feeling to me, to feel their closeness, their love.

That sweet Heavenly Nudge!

Saturday, February 25, 2012

A Heavy Heart

I am not sure what I am feeling as I write this-sadness, hurt, anxious, emptiness...a heavy heart. This day has been a day of reflection for me, I remember last year watching my son-in-law wrap my daughter's cumber bun lovingly around his waist and wear it proudly to the Justice for All Ball. Shanny had died just two weeks before the ball. What devastation and sadness filled our lives crowded our minds and completely ruled our hearts.

Still, Jas found a way to make an appearance at the Ball and carry Shanny with him by wearing the new wrap she had bought for her dress as his cumber bun. He truly is an amazing man. A year has gone by and I will be sitting with the kids again as Jas makes his way to the Ball, without Shanny, without the love of his life... with a heavy heart.

As the year came to a close, I wondered if I would feel differently, and some days I actually function pretty well. I go to work regularly, although my memory isn't great, my work is okay. I can concentrate better now and I stay on task for more than a minute or two without drifting, but there is still an emptiness inside, an untouchable place that doesn't fill back up-like a sore that just won't heal, my heart will never be the same, this feeling...a heavy heart.

I still look up at her picture and for a second or two, forget she isn't here, and then I remember and that sinking feeling comes back. The sadness is overwhelming at times, so much so that I will walk in circles until I am tired because I can't make it stop hurting and the sadness won't stop. Other days, I can look at a picture of her and see her for the beautiful young woman she was-my daughter-my angel-and blessing. Although, I must admit, I love to look at pictures of her and pretend she will call me any minute and we'll talk about something silly just like we used to do, or she'd sing to me or talk me into some outlandish shopping spree or crazy adventure...I miss those calls, I miss her-it is good to cry and let it out, but it hurts-and my heart, my heart is heavy.

I am learning to share my feelings more. When someone asks, how are you? It's really okay not to give the standard, great, how about you? Some days, I simply say-I really am okay today...other days, I may need prayer, and it is okay to ask for that. I am a pretty real person, I don't like mind games especially when it comes to grief. My grief, your grief-anyone who is grieving has enough on their plate, they don't need insincere dialog. So, I like to believe if people ask, they really want to know. Honestly, I don't always have the strength or energy to devise a clever answer, so you are going to get the real deal. My point: if you really don't want to know-don't ask; because if I am having a rough day, I'm already dealing with a heavy heart.

The sun is shining but I am not really feeling it. I will pray for the opportunity to take me beyond my grief today. God will provide He always does. Your prayer and support are always welcomed and appreciated-my family and I rely on God and friends and family a lot. For emotional support, for a smile, a kind word and a hug of understanding that this might not be a good day, we just might be dealing with a heavy heart.

What I have learned is there are no tears that God cannot dry, there is no sadness that He cannot lighten, and there is no hurt He cannot heal or spirit too broken for Him to mend. And my heart-no matter how heavy my heart-He will lovingly hold it and me in His arms and gently soothe me until I rest. In the midst of my grief, God loves my heavy heart.

Sunday, February 26, 2012

The Best Medicine

You know what cures a heavy heart? Time...And grandchildren. Today I was sad when I woke up. I thought about this day last year, the newness of being without Shanny, the rawness of the pain. The lack of understanding I had for what was happening around me and the fact that I really didn't care. This year-I cared; I just couldn't muster up the energy to drive away the sadness. And then, God spoke to my heart...

"This is a new day; breathe in the beauty of this moment. Look to the blue sky and feel the cold air on your cheeks and the warmth of the sun in the winter breeze. Know My power and My strength, but also know My love..."

After my first cup of coffee, I set about my plans for the day. Run to the bank-check. Make a Target run for the movie I wanted-check. Make sure I touched base with Jas and had the time right for sitting-check. Phone rings... Slight change in plans...

Basketball game at 5 p.m. –check... Pick up kids and take them to T's for movie and pizza-check. Run to Kim's and pick up the other little blessings to join in the fun-check. Pick up pizza and drinks-check. Let the fun begin-check!

My day had taken a change because my focus was on the present-what was happening right now-I had my daughter Tina, my son (in law) Jake and six of my eight grand blessings plus Matt, an added blessing for a night of pizza, a movie, laughter and love. This is the best medicine for a malady commonly referred to as "the blues." The joyful noise...and I do mean joyful noise those kids were making was deafening at times, but it managed to warm my heart, raise the roof and put a smile on my face. Watching them giggle, and play and be silly was absolutely wonderful. We managed to tear up a couple of pizzas, put away a 1/2 gallon of Hawaiian Punch and get in a movie too!

I was blessed because I had been given the opportunity to share the evening with my favorite little people. I am learning that getting to know my grandchildren is a blessing, not a chore. There was a time not too long ago when I would have been too busy or too tired to take on the kids and pizza and a movie. I know other grandparents did it, but I didn't. I was self-absorbed, selfish...not in the right place-whatever you want to call it-I rarely babysat and definitely not six at once.

Boy, did I miss out on a lot of fun! I am sad that Shanny did not get to see me being a real MeeMaw, that's really something that meant a lot to Shannon. She strongly believed in that bond of grandparents & grandchildren. My daughter was a very smart woman.

I could sit here and 'if only' all day but that won't change my yesterdays. I do have the chance to change today and if I am blessed, make tomorrow better.because my God loves me, flaws and all even if I am a slow learner...He gets me.

I am learning and that's what matters-lean on Him, learn every day-something, no matter how small, and know that the saying-"Time Heals", has its merits. Oh, yes-one more thing, remember-laughter, grandchildren and love- really are the best medicine!

Wednesday, February 29, 2012

Angels Two and Three

It occurred to me that I haven't really introduced you to my other two Angels...Kim and Tina. God blessed me with 3 Angels, two are here with me and one is home with her heavenly Father. Kim is in the middle and Tina is the youngest. Each one of my girls is very different from the other two in some ways, and a lot like the other two in ways close to the heart. All three love fiercely, protect their own and consider family extremely important.

They all make great friends and work hard, have a great sense of humor and love people in general. Their differences make them like night and day when it comes to cooking, going "green", politics, religion and temperament. I won't give away any secrets as to who has the bad temper or doesn't hang out in the kitchen much...I think those traits came from their father's side of the family! Just kidding, their quirks are what I love about each one of them. Each one has a very special place in my heart that belongs only to them. I know.

God blessed me because He shared three of His most precious children with me. When I think of it, I am overwhelmed by His love for me. He entrusted them to me to raise, mother, love and nurture; and when it came time - to grieve.

It has been a journey of painful love that has brought the sisters to where they are today in their walk. Both of them have become much more aware of their love for each other, and for Shanny. They both have regrets and are dealing issues of guilt. Both have come a long way in a year and both have been there for each other and me.

We each have days that we lean on one another for strength and love to get us through a particularly trying time. Out of nowhere a memory will present itself and fill us with deep regret at how we handled a situation, a squabble or disagreement. It's harder to handle now because Shanny isn't here to call and cry with, hug and ask forgiveness or be angry with, or laugh with, or kiss or any of those things we all too often take for granted with a loved one.

Do you know how many times I said-I'll call her tomorrow? I'll talk to her about it tomorrow? I'll straighten it out tomorrow? As of Feb. 10th, 2011-my tomorrows had run out with Shanny, Was I angry?

YES-with myself, with the doctors, with the nurse who wouldn't tell me Shanny was going to be alright, and with time for going too slow and going too fast all at once. But not with God..My head was spinning then and to be honest, it still spins occasionally to this day. It's still hard to believe my baby is gone.

Do you see what I just did? I was totally into Tina and Kim and our journey and just like that, I got off track. It's like that some days. I can't stay focused at all. Thank goodness, when I pray, God already knows my heart, because I'm sure I get lost in that too!

The truth is I rely very much on the girls now for support. Our journeys are different-but we have great respect for one another and we are good listeners. I don't pretend to know what it is like to lose a sibling. I am blessed God hasn't called any of my sisters or my brother home yet.

Seeing my girls ache for their sister is one of the hardest things I've had to go through-I can't fix it. I can't take their hurt away. When they were little I could hold them, rock them, soothe them and kiss it and make it better.

Now, I can listen...love them where they are and pray for them. As a mother, it doesn't seem enough. I'm sure if you have children, no matter how old they are, it doesn't matter, they are your babies. There is no feeling greater than holding them, stroking their hair and kissing their brow. I do it regularly with my girls. I am grateful they allow me to hug and kiss on them freely.

I am a very demonstrative person and need to feel and touch and smell as well as see and speak my love for them. I don't think that will ever change. I hope not. I find them both to be such miracles. Truly, I feel so blessed that God honored me to be their mother. They bring me such joy and laughter.

We talk a lot every day. Some people would say too much, but for us it works. It was the same when Shanny was here. We could talk several times a day and really not say too much. It didn't matter, we knew every call brought a smile, a giggle, a groan, smirk or WHAT NOW?!?, but we all loved each and every call, each and every day, and still do.

I have always cherished and loved my girls. I didn't always make the best decisions when it came to raising them. I hope they have forgiven me for my mistakes. I don't know that I told them enough when they were growing up how special they were to me. It does amaze me how God makes each of us in His likeness and yet each of us is uniquely beautiful whether it is the color of our eyes, or the tweak of our nose or the shape of our teeth. Our insides are ours to develop and shape. We can make them as beautiful and loving as we choose. God spoils us with gifts daily, doesn't He? Talk about your 'doting' father!

I love you Jesus. Thank you for my daily gifts and My

Angels 1, 2, 3!

Wednesday, February 29, 2012

When I close My Eyes

Gussie, Shanny's youngest ended up in the hospital with an asthma attack and a spot of pneumonia. Jason looked worn out and God bless him, he had to run home to pick up some clothes, and his laptop and some things for Gus. Poor little guy, exhausted from a long day of doctors, nurses, breathing treatments and just the general trauma of a hospital ER and admitting process, did not react well when daddy left. His grandpa greeted us with a smile. Gus red faced and wailing, sobbing for daddy looked miserable. I was reassured he was fine-just missing daddy.

Walking in on that scene stirred something in me that went against every fiber in my being. I had a very hard time seeing this little boy wrapped in his mother's blanket sobbing-inconsolably. I went to stroke his back and he withdrew and cried louder.

Realizing I was only antagonizing him, I stepped back a little, tied the balloon I brought onto his bed rail and smiled at him. He stopped for an instant and then began to cry in earnest again. Sobbing as if his world were coming to an end, he continued to rage on for another 20-30 minutes until sheer weariness overcame him. He literally cried himself to sleep. How heavy my heart was that I could not reach him. Even sadder, his mommy wasn't there to hold him, and rock him like she used to do.

It was then I realized if I closed my eyes I could almost see her there, laying next to him with her arms gently wrapped around him, snuggled in her blanket. She was stroking his back softly and gently rubbing it in between little pats. She liked to touch his fingers and cuddle with him. That is why he looked so peaceful and serene to me. Mommy was there and he felt her presence as he slept.

Sometimes, life doesn't always seem fair. I can't explain the gut wrenching pain I get when those little ones need their mommy, or when Jason looks like he needs his best friend, and that was Shannon.

Often he looks lost, sad in a way that I can't begin to explain or reach. So strong was his bond with Shanny. When this pain comes over me, the only thing I can rely on is prayer. I don't need to understand God's plan. I don't need to know the 'why' it happened. I just want to be able to give comfort to the ones that need it. So, I pray that in my weakness, I find strength: Strength to reach beyond myself and touch a little one's heart with the love of a grandma. Or I am able to offer some comfort to my son (in law) when he is hurting by a word or touch. I know that if I ask God will provide the means.

When I close my eyes, my world shows me a different reality. It shows me if I believe that God truly watches over us and loves us-He will never let His children suffer needlessly. He does provide their mommy, sometimes in the dreams of a child when their world can be perfect. Sometimes, in a letter she has written if she is far away. sometimes, on the telephone or the other end of a computer. But, God does provide. So, when I close my eyes, I see Shanny with her kids on the couch, with her blanket, cuddling, laughing, loving..she is only a thought away-when I close my eyes.

Friday, March 2, 2012

Ask and It Shall Be Given To You

I am not sure if that is the correct verse but I know it is

something similar. I always said it like this, 'Ask and you shall

receive.' It was just easier for me to understand. The part that

isn't so easy is the receiving. Prayers go up and answers come, but

the answers aren't always what we think they should be.

Sometimes, the answers aren't even close to what we asked for in

our prayer. I must admit, it doesn't always sit well with me.

I like to think my faith is strong. Yet, there are days when

my faith is sorely tested. Those tests come in all forms. Our

responses can either strengthen our faith or dissolve it. Usually, if

I am perplexed by a situation and I don't understand the response

to it-I pray. I quit praying for understanding. Now, I pray for

acceptance. I learned a long time ago..God knows best. Just

because I don't understand His plan is okay, I can't see the grand picture He has in mind. But I do know when He unveils that picture to me; I will again be in awe of His artistry.

When I say some things test me, I mean it comes in all sizes and forms. For instance, the news can be a great source of confusion and doubt. A story about a family comes on the news. Mother, father and a four year old are going to hospital to pick up healthy newborn and bring home. Should be a joyful event, right? For everyone, parents, sibling, grandparents...well, a major accident occurs, mother and father and sibling are killed, newborn survives. The 18 year old that crossed the line and killed them, worked with the mother of the children. How does such a beautiful story turn so tragic? How do we begin to explain it? How do we not say-Why did God let this happen?

Think of the devastation and pain. The grandparent's everyday will be reminded of their son or daughter, and their grandchild, because they are raising the surviving infant. The young girl will live with the guilt of the accident for the rest of her life, no matter what the circumstances were-she survived, that alone will cause her guilt.

There are other situations that create a shift in faith or an inkling of doubt. Things like a bad break-up, a job loss, or divorce. These are all events that can lead to shaky ground but nothing like death of a loved one. Nothing has plunged me so deeply into indescribable pain. Physical pain, that left me wailing and wanting to bang my head on a wall to relieve the pain in my heart.

After weeks of numbness and fits of tears, came days of listless, uncaring existing from one moment to the next, not feeling anything and not wanting to, almost adjusting to the weariness and dense fog of shock. The pain would momentarily dissipate until I remembered my daughter died.

Then I was washed with grief and drowning in gut wrenching sadness and the feeling that someone had ripped my heart out or worse, had ripped only part of it out, and I was forced to live without the rest of my heart and there was nothing I could do to fix it.

What about my other two girls? How can I heal their pain? I can't stand to see them suffer and hurt and grieve for their sister. I cannot fix this. This is a mother's job. This is what I do. I fix things.

Only this time, I can't. I have to give it to God. I have to know He will cradle my baby, and love her and stroke her head, and sing to her. He will do all these things and more. He created her. He loves her. He grieves with me and for me. He loves me. He wipes my tears and gently leads my way through this darkness.

Prayer, in whatever form is truly our communication with God, Our Father. He will provide. He listens and He hears, and He answers. Will it always be what we think we want? Probably not. Will it always be when we want it? I doubt it. But this I know is true-God is a keeper of His promise; He will not fail us nor forsake us, ever. So, ask and you shall receive. My prayer, is always, Lord let Your will be done and let my will be Your will and let me set about Your work today with a happy heart. Amen

I don't need to understand, I just need to accept. God knows we are hurting. He knows each one of our hearts. He knows our needs and our desires. If we believe in Him, then we trust He will do what is best for us. It isn't always easy and it isn't always what I think I want or need. But deep down, I know it what's best.

Today I have experienced so many different emotions. I have been sad, happy, peaceful, restless, anxious, weary and so very grateful. I miss my Shanny, I want to hug her and feel her close to me again. It feels like a lifetime ago that I hugged her. That is so painful, it is such an emptiness that nothing will fill up. So for now I will pray...

I spent time with my sisters and family last evening-we were celebrating John's birthday. There was so much love in my sister's house, I could feel it everywhere. I am so keenly aware of my feelings now that I experience everything at a heightened level. That may sound a little crazy but I think my need to emote went into overdrive after I lost Shanny. There was a sense of deep love awakened in me that I had let go dormant for a long time. I had become comfortable in my daily routine of family, kids, grand kids, work, weekends, work, etc. My mind had become absorbed with "too much life in too little time."

After I regained my ability to think and comprehend and care, after Shanny died-I had a new perspective on life. I cry now, some days, wail for a day, to show her I have learned how to love more and think less. But my time for that is not now, but I have faith that one day I will share my lesson with her, I will hold her and say all the things a mother should say to her daughter, but for now..I pray.

I ask My Father to guide me in my steps daily because my steps are shaky and I am weak. I am nothing without Him. I am grateful, so very grateful He holds me in His hands and shelters and protects me. He has dried many a tear, and wiped my face, kissed my brow and lovingly soothed my tantrums of grief. He knows my pain-He gave His son.

Tonight I went to a benefit for a brother of a friend. The family had planned this benefit and he was called home before it took place. We gathered and caught up with friends and had a great evening. David had a wonderful idea. If we all gathered and broke bread and supported the grieving family, wouldn't that make life so much easier? I asked if that isn't what funerals were all about. His response was -"No, not really". They are sad and solemn, we are happy and celebrating. This is how it should be. I love that outlook and I agree with him. But it isn't that easy when you are the one grieving. The pain is so intense; you hardly notice friends and family for a while. And so for now I pray...

I pray for direction and strength. I pray that God somehow uses me to reach others in their grief. He has been my rock and I want to share that with people, His Hope. So I will pray.

I want to remember Shannon for the beautiful young woman she was wife, mother, daughter, sister, and friend. She filled so many roles and touched so many lives. I don't want to forget. Lord, I don't want others to forget her either. I don't always understand how other people can go on with their life and how life just keeps happening all around me, except it doesn't for me. It came to a screeching halt on Feb. 10, 2011. It has taken its toll on me. Father, I am tired and my energy wanes. So, for now I pray...

I pray that if I choose to visit the past that I will be strong enough to leave once my visit comes to an end. I don't want to live there, in the past. But now, Shannon is part of the past, because she is not present. So, how can I lovingly make her a part of my present and future? That thought hurts, Lord. I can barely stand to utter the words. So, I will pray.

I can carry her with me in memory and honor her memory by dealing with some of the grief and sharing Your love with others. I wish to smile, to sing or whistle a tune, to whisper a prayer and shout His glory. But all of this takes strength and courage and I still need time to heal, Lord. So, I will pray..

I will take each day as it comes, Lord. Honor you always and in the midst of my grief I will find the joy you have blessed us with in the day. And if it eludes me til night, I will embrace the challenge in searching it out. That takes perseverance, Lord so for now I will pray.

I will work towards finding You always in the midst of my busy-ness. I will try to do Your will with a happy heart and accept today for what it is, a new day, a beginning...Ahh, Lord I need to pray.

I want to thank You Lord for your love and mercy. Your unyielding strength and light into my darkness. You, Father are my everything, my world and I just want to honor and glorify You always with my words, my thoughts, and my actions, but I am human Lord, and I crumble and I fall. I get lost and I get sad. I forget sometimes, in my grief that You are there and You love me..I forget because my hurt overwhelms me, but You already know this, You created me. You are there every time I call Your name-in the early morning hours, in the darkest time of night-You are ever present on this journey of grief-with me, alongside me and some days-holding me up. And so, Lord-I will pray. Today, this very moment I am glad to be alive. I am resting in the peace You have provided me.

For now...

Child's Play

I was thrilled after church when my grandson of four said..I want to go with MeeMaw. You see, since Momma died, he hasn't left daddy's side for long. Usually, he refuses my invitations to play but today he was asking to come with me!

Church had its rough moments for the kids. Children's Liturgy keeps them busy but it seems as though the minute we are back in the pew, their little minds just wander. Gus usually wants whatever he isn't supposed to have at the moment and gets progressively louder if you refuse to give it to him. Jas somehow manages to maintain his cool and get through the last blessing and we are out the door!

Today was no different except today I had prayed for direction. I was happy to be at church actually. I had called Jas earlier and was going to beg off service, I had a sinus headache and wasn't feeling well, but I could hear Evie on the phone and when Jas said, we're going, MeeMaw, are you? I heard Evie in the background when I said yes, I'll be there-whoop and yeah! That made my heart so happy...I didn't care what was hurting; I was going to church with a happy heart!

I always arrive about 15 minutes before Mass starts, I like the quiet. I like to talk to God freely, just me and Him, one on one. I really like my "me" time with Him. Sunday I asked Him if He could guide me to do His will with the kiddos. I am not exactly, grandmotherly, all the time. I don't always relate too well in certain situations and I admit I don't have all the answers as to how to handle kids nowadays. I respect Jason so much; I would never do anything without asking him first anyway. I just feel like I am not always much in the way of help or guidance for him, not that he needs it.

Anyway, I prayed that God would direct me to help Jas with the kids more. Give him some relief, and at the same time reach the kids so they would be more comfortable with me. I love them all so much, I just don't always know exactly how to show it. Is Our Father not an Awesome God? I gave Him my concerns, and

He knew my heart, and gave me the opportunity to spend time with little Gus. It just doesn't get better, and yet it did!

After I got Gus' things from the car, car seat, cup, blanket-check! Off we went on our adventure..first words from Gus-"MeeMaw, do you have an X-Box 360?" I thought I might be in trouble for a minute...

"No, Gus.."

"Do you have other games?"

" What kind of games?"

"For a 'puter?"

"I have a computer, Gus."

"But do you have a 'puter like my dad lets me play?"

"No, Gus..I don't have that kind."

"Well, do you have any kid games? "

"Gus, we will have to use our imagination."

"MeeMaw, is PaPa home?"

This is the part where I usually get my feelings hurt. Every time I am with the little critters, they always ask where their PaPa is. Now, mind you, I am the one that usually takes them to the movies, or babysits, or takes crafts to their house, or pizza and a movie. Still, is PaPa home...I just don't get it.

We burst into the house and Gus went in search of his PaPa. Sierra, our 95 lb. puppy greeted him with lots of wet kisses first. PaPa heard the commotion and came out of the back room, where I know he was watching golf, even though he told me he was busy making plans on how to clean out the garage and basement in the Spring. As soon as Gus saw him, the smile lit up his face. And Gus was happy, too! Gussie announced he was hungry and PaPa promised to make him a sandwich after we went next door to visit Aunt T-T and Olivia. Once next door, Gus found Olivia's toys a little more entertaining than our house. But Olivia wasn't really in the mood to share. Being not quite two, the concept of sharing is still new and within minutes Gus announced-MeeMaw, can we go back to your house? So much for Weebles and the new Tree house!

As soon as we got in the house, Gus decided we should play tents and hide and seek. This is a game where you stuff a 56 year young woman under a blanket, two feet off the floor and repeatedly tell her to pull in her feet, because they are stickin' outta the tent! The tent being a cherished blankie of Momma's draped over the arm of the couch, the chair arm and the ottoman. Now, PaPa had to "find" us hiding several times and after I took my turn at locating PaPa and Gus in their tent.

Gus remembered he was hungry.

Pa took a break to make us some Cream Cheese toast with chocolate milk and turn on one of Gussie's channel nine favorites. All was good in the Lohse household.. Before too long, Gus wanted to see some action. How about the park? The toy store? And if that store doesn't have enough toys, we can go to another store, right? We decided since it was beginning to drizzle outside and it was rather chilly, we would save the park for another day, and head for the $1 Store.

That is such a funny concept to me! The $1 Store. I have yet to go into one and spend $1! I don't think I ever leave without dropping at least $20 or more. But as we all scoured the shelves, row after row, for just the right special toy. Gus informed me-

He needed a teddy bear because he had one and it needed a friend. His sister would love the pink squishy elephant. It's pink!

He needed a new foam dart gun-'cause he kept losing his darts. The one with two guns-not one. J-Bug would like one too, but he only needs one gun. Evie would like the sand art kit, too, and Jason would like it too, cause he lost one of his bottles.

That's so nice of you, to think of your brother and sister...

Then, he saw another toy he really liked...I think Evie

would really like this basketball game, too, MeeMaw..

Well, then we have to put something else back.

But she would like them both..

We need to pick just one, Gus..

After about another 1/2 hour or so we had finally made all

our selections and we were checking out when he said,"Now, can

we go to the park?" PaPa and I smiled at each other and loaded

him in the car. What a perfect day! Simple and yet so very

perfect. I still smile when I think of some of our conversations that

day. Gus in all of his 4 years, managed to brighten my day in a big

way! Just be being the sweet little boy that he is...

God really is good; He listens and hears our prayers. He

knows our hearts so well. I am so grateful for the gifts He gives me

each and every day, the gifts of a wonderful husband, who has

taken on the role of a PaPa, beautifully and lovingly, my 8 little

blessings, my grandchildren, who bring smiles to my face with their

hugs and kisses.

A few years ago, I didn't appreciate those simple gestures of love, but I am learning, Lord, don't give up on me...my daughters, who love me in spite of the mistakes I made as a mom without all the right answers and making some pretty poor choices, co-workers and a job that allows me to work with others, and service our Veterans. Friends who know me and love me anyway!

Today, God taught me a new lesson- How to find Joy and Peace... And it was Child's Play!

Friday, March 9, 2012

All Wrapped Up

I prayed for direction...and I got it. I wanted a sign from Shanny, and I felt her presence and her spirit. Sunday was such an amazing day with Gussie and all. So, when Wednesday came I said a quick prayer. Lord, let me be patient. I am going to see the kids for a craft night, sand art and American Idol. But for me, it is so much more. I pray on it daily. I ask for direction and guidance about how to be a good grandma and how to step up and help Jason without stepping on his toes.

This is a real blessing for me and I am excited! God gets me, and I am grateful for that.,.while some may not understand my constant prayer for direction-the Lord does. He knows I wasn't always Grandma of the year. There was a time, not too long ago, when I was too old, too busy, or too tired. That was the litany of my excuses, take your pick.

I am not proud of my recent past (within the last few years I have made an effort to be more engaged.) but it is, nonetheless, the truth. The truth? I was very self-absorbed. I was single, over 50, had a very active social life and wasn't really aware of the necessity to cultivate a rigorous grandma appeal with my 8 little blessings. I do accept responsibility for that now.

I was also unattached...That has changed and I am very happily married to a wonderful man with a heart of gold...who gets me, craziness and all! He knows my heart and my intentions are good, if not a little misguided at times. He knows I love my daughters passionately, and would gladly have changed places with my daughter Shannon. He also knows that my faith has made this journey of grief survivable for me. Without God and faith-I have nothing. I am nothing.

I loved hearing Evie screech, "MeeMaw's here!" before she peeked out the window and opened the door. I was welcomed with a big Eva hug and smile. Those moments are so very special to me. Not too far behind is Gus, "hey, MeeMaw...Can we do our craft now?" His excitement at my visit brings a smile to my face. I waited all day for this.

Thank You, Lord, for these magical moments in my day. I feel Shanny in these moments. I feel her presence, her spirit, her closeness and her guidance. I want to take a moment and thank you and Glorify You for this and so much more, Lord!

JD is on the couch watching TV and he smiles as I come into the room. "MeeMaw I got my spacers-see?" He opens wide and sure enough, there they are blue spacers in his teeth. "WOW! Did that hurt?" We talked about his braces and then moved on to his homework which was about Boas and Pythons. In my best grandma voice I said, snakes are very interesting creatures, aren't they? (Inside my skin is crawling, I really don't like snakes...) So, about the sand art bottles...

After doing a sun catcher with Evie, 3 sand art bottles with green, blue, orange and pink sand and three budding artists, we sat down to American Idol. Before we knew it our evening was winding.down. But not before I got a few good snuggles, some race car driving with Gus, a good back scratching with JD, and a promise from Evie for a girl's day out! We made plans for Jason's concert the next evening and PaPa arrived within a few minutes.

Before I left for the evening, Gus brought me his Momma's blanket, we snuggled and as I gathered him in my arms and held him, wrapped in his Momma's love-I could feel her with me. When I closed my eyes, I could breathe in her sweetness. I miss her. I know she is watching over her little ones, and one grandma who is learning..

My heart filled with love for my grand children, their mother and You, Lord. You have us all wrapped in Your blanket of love. Thank you for the comforting warmth. You provide when I am cold with sadness and grief. Thank You for Your forever love.

"Good Morning, sweetie."

"Mom?"

"Yes, it's me. I missed you so much I invented this Angelograph."

"Great, Mom. I miss you all, too. But God really has it all covered. I mean-everything."

"Well, that may be so, but we miss you terribly, and until He accepts my suggestion for a visiting day where we can come and visit or vice versa, this Angelograph will have to do."

"Mom, you do know what Faith is, right?"

"Are you getting smart with your mother?"

"No, Mom. I just mean if you say you believe in God and His will be done then..."

"Shanny, if you only knew how much I see you in your babies' eyes, and sometimes what I see is such sadness and longing. Maybe, I imagine it, but I don't think so. Those kids really miss you. You are their mommy. And what about Jason, he grieves for his best friend. He still doesn't really smile with his whole body and heart anymore. I see it. Oh, he moves his mouth and it looks like a smile, but it really isn't from his heart."

"Mom, mom...I get it."

"You are still impatient with me, Shanny. You should work on that."

"Mom, I am with my babies. You said it the other day. You feel me sometimes. It's because I am there. My spirit is with them, bringing them comfort. I often visit Jason, too. Believe me, Mom. My love reaches from heaven all the way to Pernod Avenue and my house, too."

"So, when I am in my car driving and a little voice says...Go ahead, run that red light."

"NO. Mom...that is not me. I may have gotten a few speeding tickets, but I would not tell you to run a red light. Unless, it is a red light camera...I don't agree with those."

"A few, Shanny? - A few speeding tickets?"

"Mom, what I am saying is...when you are sad, I am there to wipe your tears. Just like when you were there for me. And when, you want to give up, I am the little voice urging you on. Because I know you can do it, Mom. You are so strong."

"I wasn't though, Shanny – I wasn't always there to wipe your tears. We weren't always close. I am so very sorry for some of the choices I made."

"Me, too Mom, I love you...and when you feel a little tickle...it's an Angel hug. Our wings tend to tickle a little."

"You know, I feel better, Shan. This Angelograph might just do the trick."

"Mom, don't you think that is really His job?"

"Well, if that were so, Shanny, then how am I having this conversation with you?"

"Shanny?"

"Baby? Good morning? Why the big smile?" David was waking me gently.

"It's nothing. David, where is my Angelograph?"

"Your what?"

(Tickle, tickle.).

Tuesday, March 13, 2012

In My Dreams

Sunday was a beautiful day of reflection with a group of ladies at Vianney High School. It was a day of fellowship, renewal of spirit, and communion with the Lord. It just doesn't get any better than that. I met some incredible women and spent time with God one-on-One. It was a day to remember. It gave me strength and courage and a smile! Did you ever hear a priest or minister speak and you felt like what they were saying was meant just for you? That is what I felt like all day. It was as if God said to him, there is this lady who will be there...she lost her daughter last year and she is suffering, console her.

His words lifted me up.

Monday came and the day dawned.. What a beautiful day greeted me. God sure does know how to bless us, doesn't He? The birds were singing, the air was clean and fresh. The sun was warm on my face. I felt a sense of renewal. When I got to work all was good. Nothing was going to dampen my spirit today. And I think it made my day that much more productive. I prayed throughout the day like I always do for people that need it as the day goes on, someone is ill, or someones child needs a prayer, a neighbor, and coworker, friend, pet or family member. We had chocolate cake so that deserved a prayer of thanks!

Prayer is always part of my day and it keeps me going. It's amazing how it touches so many facets of my day.

That evening I exercised with my daughter, so there was a prayer said. Believe me..I prayed. Then, I relaxed with my hubby and again prayed for the days events. Finally, before I closed my eyes, I prayed for peaceful sleep and thanked the Lord for my blessings. What a beautiful night's sleep I had in store.

Sometime during the night, my Angel came to me in my dreams. There she was, huggable, kissable, and in my heart I could feel her presence. We were with her children visiting. We were on the couch and I couldn't stop touching her. It was as if I knew she wasn't going to be with me forever, and yet she seemed to be oblivious to our situation. I was jabbering away and talking about anything and everything. She was actually becoming a little annoyed with me. Of course, she was busy entertaining and keeping an eye on the kids. They didn't seem to be aware of our time restraints either.

It seemed to be getting dark outside and she was getting tired. The kids were quieting down and I was just not ready to go. I wanted to talk some more, about anything. I just wanted to hear her voice, feel her touch, and be close to her. Shanny had this way of running her hands through her hair and pulling it back as if it were bothering her when she was getting frustrated. I think she was almost at that point. I finally asked her what was wrong and she said,

"Mom, I'm tired." I looked at her with a shocked kind of surprised look, and said...I just want to make the most of our time, to talk and catch up...

She looked at me like I had two heads and said;" Can't you use the telephone?"

I was so surprised by her answer, I woke straight up!

Now, I am thinking...the Angelograph didn't really work out so well, could the Angelophone be any better?

Dreams are a way of connecting with our loved ones. I'm sure my missing Shanny so much brought us closer in my dream. She was so very real, I wanted to hold her forever and not wake up. The funny thing was she had no idea what I was experiencing in the dream. It was like part of me was still in reality, knowing she wasn't here, and part of me wanted to believe she was.

When I woke up, I felt her love all around me. I went to work happy and shared my dream with a coworker. I had wanted to dream of Shanny. Tina told me she had Shanny come to her in a dream and it comforted her a great deal. The sadness is, once you are awake, you have to deal with reality. The pain will return, and the emptiness and the gaping hole where she belongs are present again. But you have a piece of her you didn't have yesterday. At least, it feels like you do, even if it is only in my dreams.

Thank you, Lord, for the gift of dreams. They bring us a lightness of heart that we might be seeking. Thank you, Lord, for the gift of sleep. It gives our bodies and our minds much needed rest from the days labor and thought.

Thank you, Lord, for Your very presence in my life. You are the reason for my lightness of heart, my ability to sleep and desire to rest at the end of our day. Let my first waking thought be of You and my last thought of each day be for Your mercy and Your grace. In Your Precious Son's Most Holy Name, I will Pray, again and if it be Your will. Again and again -Amen.

Friday, March 16, 2012

Signs of Spring

I can feel her in the air! It is fresh and dewy. The air is warm and when the sun is shining is it actually hot on my skin. Flowers are just beginning to bloom. Trees are budding and the earth is bursting with colors of Spring. This is Shanny's time! Heaven must be getting quite a garden this year...

A year of adjustment has gone by. It seems almost too hard to believe. The Spring passed into Summer last year and before I knew it, Fall was upon us and then Winter. The Holidays were a blur. And, here we are again. I wonder if this year will bode differently. I wonder if I will feel the air and see the flowers and smell Spring? I guess it is in my choosing.

I heard the rain beating on the roof and then the windows. The spattering lulled me into a sense of melancholy laziness. Time makes me think too much. Sometimes that is not a good thing. I miss Shannon so much it hurts.

The pain causes me to become agitated and angry because I cannot control it and I cannot change it. I forget the moments of peacefulness; I can't recall the warmth of God's touch at this time. I feel empty and alone and sad. I want my daughter back.

These days don't come as often as they used to in the beginning. It has been over a year of painful miserable days mixed with days of bearable, I can get through this, I know she is in Heaven days.

This just happens to be a dark, sad "why" day. This is how quickly my moods can change from understanding God's will to not caring what He wants, I want my daughter, to if I pray more and harder and longer and beg God more. But my world is forever changed. My life will never be the same and coming to terms with that takes time.

Staying busy usually helps keep my mind off of the devastating pain. I can function at a level that most would think I am coping very well. They don't live inside me. They don't think my thoughts; feel my pains or dream of seeing my baby again. I close my eyes and want to breathe her in. I settle for a memory of her scent. I walk about the room touching things that belonged to her, remind me of her, pictures of her. A card she wrote me. I listen to her voice on an old recorded work message. I play a video with her in it and make believe she is still here. Some days I can actually fool myself if I don't talk to anyone for a while. I can stay in bed, shut out the world and refuse the truth. But not forever, because I have two other children, a husband and eight grandchildren who love me and need me to live, to love them like I did before.

No, life isn't easy now. But I have a choice. Do I ignore the signs of spring or do I choose life? What will I do? I will pray. The power of prayer and my faith have brought me to this day. Thank God for His mercy and His love. He understands my pain and hears my prayers. He will give me comfort in my storm. Even the storm of my grief

Sunday, March 18, 2012

My 8ᵗʰ Little Blessing

Olivia...My 8th Little Blessing! Today is her 2nd
Birthday! That's right; two years ago today I got a call at work...

"Mom, could you take me to the hospital...just to get
checked out?" What mother would refuse their daughter that
request?

Once we arrived there was a whirlwind of activity and Tina
was staying; unlike when I was in labor years ago. In today's world
if you are dilated to a 3, they keep you. It was a long day for Tina
and Jacob, but once the decision was made-we knew we were
having a baby...a St. Patty's Day baby!

Last year came and went and honestly, I know I celebrated
Olivia's first birthday, but I remember little of it. I was in the
protective cocoon God wraps us in when we first lose a loved one.
I was basically numb and in shock. Physically, I may have been
present but I was emotionally not available. Even after I returned

to work in April, I wasn't really functioning at full capacity, but I was trying.

This year, I was very present for LuLu's birthday. I was invited to spend the day and I pretty much did. I shopped for Olivia and decided on the prettiest little dress and sweater. Shanny would have approved. Funny, but it seems as though when I shop she is with me...guiding me, taking me to the right clothes, picking out what she would have if she was here. I feel her closeness and I find it very comforting.

Even though I was sad, Shanny was urging me to go on and enjoy the day. She was almost pushing me. Once I got to Tina's, it went a little better. Tina had a rough morning. She wasn't in much better spirits than I was and if it hadn't been for LuLu treating us to a floor show of her playing her guitar and being silly...and being one sweet birthday girl, I don't know if we would have snapped out of it.

The smile on her just melts my heart. Jake and Tina went shopping and Jake's mom came over and we watched Lu together for a while. Micki took some pictures and we played and talked and Lu entertained us both with her dancing and playful nature. Between chasing the dog around the house and playing peek-a-boo in her tunnel, we had a grand time.

This is how God works. He knows who we need, when we need them and how to heal our brokenness, even if it is just for a while. He gives us the gift of joy. Whether it is through our grandchildren or a friend, or a church service, or an Al-Anon meeting, He has the answer to our needs. We only need to ask.

And so it was, Olivia on her 2nd Birthday gave ME a Gift! She gave me the gift of pure, unconditional, love. I hope someday I can thank Jesus in person for letting me come to this party!

For now, I will pray.

Thank you, Jesus, -for my family and my friends who love me where I am, happy or sad. Thank you for Your constant love and mercy. Thank You for Your many Gifts, Lord. Especially My 8th Little Blessing!

Tuesday, March 20, 2012

The Most Important Words I'll Ever Speak

I spoke a lot of words today...

but none so important as

Thank You, Lord!

Thank you for the puffy blue clouds

-so I can play, 'Do you see what I see?'

Thank you for the tiny flower buds

that peek out of the garden.

Thank you for the birds

that have made a home in our birdhouse.

Thank you for the new buds

on the trees I planted.

Thank you for the rabbits

and the squirrels,

pesty little critters that they be.

Thank you for my wind chimes

that play such beautiful music.

Thank you for the warmth of sunshine that dries my tear

streaked cheeks.

Thank you for your gentleness

it soothes my wounded heart.

Thank you for my family

who love me in my brokenness.

Thank you for my friends

who know me and love me anyway.

Thank you for my morning coffee

it starts my day with a smile.

Thank you for my Facebook Friends

who lift my spirits

with a kind word of encouragement, whether they know me

or not.

Thank you for my dog

who loves me with her wet nose and wagging tail.

Thank you for my cat

who greets me with a snuggle and a purr when I get up in

the morning.

Thank you for my work buddies,

who bring chocolate...just because.

Thank you for my children

the greatest gift a mother could receive.

Thank you for my 8 Little Blessings, their hugs are filled

with the best, most rewarding love of all;

they love me just because I am me.

Thank you for a husband

who knows when to smile and say..."Sure, Honey.

Whatever you think is best."

Thank you for letting me wake up and pray...

Thank you, Lord, for another day to praise and glorify

Your name.

Let me do Your will and make it my own with a smile in my

heart

and kind words for the people I meet along my way today.

Thank you always,

for the gift of Your Son...

who gave His life for me so that one day I may say to You

lovingly,

face-to-heavenly face

Thank You, Lord!

Thursday, March 22, 2012

God's Love Fills Me Up

I know this may all sound crazy. I am grieving over the loss of my daughter but I am learning how God fills me up with the love of my family.

I could beat myself up about not learning this lesson while Shanny was here. She wanted so much to see me be a real grandma. I wasn't ready then. I was still trying to find me in all of my ignorance. I hadn't reached out to the Lord totally. I hadn't let go, and I hadn't held on.

I was on the fence about my faith, my beliefs, my worth and my value to God or anyone else. How could my being a grandma really matter? But to Shanny it did. I couldn't see what she saw...I couldn't see the smile of the child that would warm my heart, or the tear that would break my heart. I couldn't grasp the strength in the hand of the child, or the gentle hug that would give me strength. Shanny knew. She tried to tell me. I wouldn't listen. I was busy, tired, or found an excuse. But Shanny tried. I love her for trying. I hope she loves me for finally learning. I am getting it and loving it!

Shared an evening in the park with 7 out of 8 of my little Blessings, my Angel #2 and My son (in law). We had such fun! I'm not sure who was more exhausted by the end of the evening-the kids or us! We ran, we rolled, we jumped, we climbed, we flew and we crept...and then we did it again!

It was Evie's 8th Birthday and she got her ears pierced...big girl. She is a beautiful girl with a spirit to match. She reminds me of her mama. I love the way she is who God has made her to be! She loves hard, plays hard and when she lets you into her heart and shares her little self, she has beautiful thoughts and ideas. She has helped me in my journey. Evie shared with me her secrets on how to handle some of my anger issues. Good stuff, Evie. She teaches me when I am with her, as do all my grand-Angels, about God's pure love and His ability to heal through time and fill me up with His goodness by opening my heart to my grandchildren and accepting their gifts of unconditional love.

There is something so special about holding a child's hand and hearing them sing...one,two,three...swing me, grandma! It melts my heart every time...

I watched them on the playground with other kids and thought, what a fine job their parents are doing. They all played with other kids, shared nicely, took turns and watched out for each other. My heart was overflowing with love and warmth.

Through my grief and sadness-God provides. He teaches me daily through others, especially the children, for they are pure of heart. His love is endless and His mercy is great!

We celebrated Evie's birthday with cupcakes at her school, a few gifts from family and friends, new pierced ears...but I am the one who received a beautiful gift. Another cherished memory to tuck away.

Thank you, Lord. Your love fills me up and my heart overflows! Today I will be grateful for this hectic chaos. It is grand! I will relish the craziness and the fun! I will remember my youth and linger in the past a moment or two, breathe deeply of the scent of childhood and what memories are there. I will praise You for the goodness of my children and my grand children. They are so precious to me, Lord. Thank you, for your patience with me in realizing my priorities. Thank you for not giving up on me but for providing me with opportunities to grow in the art of being a "good grandma."

Thank you for the blessings you send me each and every day, Lord...in the form of daily life.

Lord, I pray for the day when I might see You and bow before Your Heavenly throne and thank you for Your very special love and how You filled me up!

Wednesday, March 28, 2012

Prayer in the Sunshine State

WOW!! I just got back in town from visiting my sister, Jan in Naples, Florida. What a wonderful visit! My sister Geri and I flew out for a few days this past week. The sun, the air, foliage and wildlife are amazing. What a place for prayer! Every breath I took reminded me to be thankful for the air I breathe.

The sweetness of the gulf breeze filled the air with goodness. The flowers in bloom scented the air with a clean and fresh Florida-only aroma. The night sky seemed clearer and the stars sparkled like diamonds against the inky black night. The moon's glow was warm and soft and the planets were visible with my own eyes, another of God's masterpieces.

Every palm tree swaying in the breeze played a song of beauty that seemed as though it was playing just for us. When I saw the shadow of the palm fronds on the green grass carpet, they appeared like angel wings fluidly in motion. What beauty God allows our eyes to feast on.

When I entered her church I was greeted with a smile and warm welcome. The choir sang and the words melted my heart. The music was magical. My spirit was soaring as I left the church. On Sunday, a Jamaican choir sang for us and I cannot tell you how their music wrapped my heart in God's love. The words, the beat of the music and the vocals were food for my hungry soul. I kept beat with childlike awe as the music lifted me up to praising I hadn't felt in a long time. God's peace and spirit filled the church and I wept with the joy of the experience. It was beautiful...

Then, I sat back and remembered I had shared time in Florida with Kim, my middle Angel, and Tina my youngest Angel...but not Shannon. Somehow, we never had the time or our schedules did not mesh and we never shared the sand at the beach or the moonlight...I missed her. I longed to share these moments with her and knew physically that would not ever happen. My heart began to break into a thousand little pieces with the knowledge of lost time.

I quietly prayed for the strength I needed to accept that reality. But God had a different plan. His plan wasn't that Shannon would physically share this time with me, but that spiritually I would feel her presence and be filled with a love only He could provide. So, as I walked the beach with my sister, Shannon was also playing in the gentle waves. And as I watched a gorgeous orange sunset, Shannon witnessed God's artwork across the Florida sky. And as I coaxed a shy little duck for the camera, Shanny giggled with me later, when my sister announced...those ducks will follow anyone, Rosie...here I thought I was the "duck whisperer."

Every memory that was created, every prayer that was uttered, and every hug that was shared...Shanny was a part of it. My Heavenly Father gave me that gift, because that is what I needed. When I prayed in the Prayer Garden at Jan's church, I wanted so much to reach beyond my own selfish desires. But truth be told, I missed my baby and asked God to provide for me a way to share this all with her. And, He graciously did just that. How wondrous is He?

I cannot begin to tell you how much love I have felt this past week. From my sisters, from Jan's church family, from My Heavenly Father, and Shanny...we left our own footprints in the sand, just as Christ so often leaves His prints upon my heart. Thank you, Father...again and again.

Saturday, March 31, 2012

Missing You

There is no rhyme or reason; I am missing you today, your smile, and your sweetness, your voice. You...

I cannot begin to explain how or what I was thinking when all of a sudden, you were on my mind and I would not stop thinking of you. I wanted so badly to wrap my arms about you and just hold you. I miss you, daughter. It is at times like this when my faith is sorely tested. I lean on God for strength, for I know there is no answer to my question, just as there is no reason for what happened on Feb. 10, 2011.

I don't have the tightness in my chest any more when I think of that day. I know God has you in His arms. I no longer grapple with your last moments...I gave that to the Lord, too. He comforted you in your last moments. You felt His touch before you felt your life end; I know that to be true. I believe.

As you took your last breath of this life, you took your first breath of eternal life, and that is how God gently escorts us from this world to Heaven. I do wonder what your first sight of Heaven looked like though. Who or what did you see first? Did you first see the face of your loving Christ or did you seek out your Grandmother or Pa first?

I prayed that you were at peace when you left this life; not in pain or fear. I prayed that Angels were sent to meet you and that no harm or darkness overcame you. I prayed that your final thoughts of this world were knowing you were loved. I prayed that you would see your children remember you in prayer each night, and your husband speak of you with love and respect. I prayed that you would join us at family gatherings as we praise God for His blessings and you would feel our love among the clouds and stars. I prayed that the Angels would wipe away your tears with their robes of gold and tickle you with their feathery wings. I prayed you would visit me in my dreams and feel my kisses on your cheek. I prayed for your forgiveness for my shortcomings as a mother. I prayed you'd love me still after you saw the heavenly greeters and remembered my last words, I love you.

I cannot hold onto the memories without tears and I cannot let go. I cannot touch your face or feel your sweet embrace, and I cannot forget our last hug and kiss. I wish I had spent more time with you the night before your test. I wish I had spent the night. I wish I had come earlier in the day. I wish I had told you to put it off. I wish I had been a better mom. I wish...

Times like these, I wish I could make it all go away. I wish I could wake up and it would never have ever happened and I wish I could make it all disappear and I wish I was magic and I wish I was God and I wish...What? What do I wish?

Through this nightmare of grief-God has held my hand and my heart. He has wiped my tears and carried me when I was too weak to walk.He hears me when I am sad. He hears me when I am angry. He listens to my ramblings. He listens to my rants. He rocks me when I go to Him for comfort. He soothes me with sleep if I am tired. He knows my needs and my true desires. He knows my grief. He, too, suffers with me, for He too gave His Son - for me. What love has He, what unconditional, unending, everlasting, all powerful love? And Jesus? He knew He would suffer and die for my sins. And He honored His Father's will. Who am I to question Him?

Thank you, Father for the Gift of Your Son, Jesus. Thank you for the gift of my daughter, Shannon. Thank you for the gift of life everlasting. Thank you for Your love and mercy. Thank you for each new day, a beginning; and the dusk; a time to rest in the knowledge of Your saving grace. And thank You, Father most of all for my gift of faith.

Tuesday, April 3, 2012

My Easter Angel

This week gives me a lot of food for thought, a lot of reason to pray, a lot of time to think, a lot of tears to shed, and most of all, a chance to praise God for His Son, for sharing My Easter Angel, Shanny with me for 34 years and for the power of prayer and faith...

I am seeing so much this week, God is opening my eyes and my heart to others in a way that I have not experienced for a while. Spring is in the air and flowers are blooming in mass, colors are vibrant and my heart still aches for my child, who lays in the earth this day. She will not rise this Sunday. He will-and that gives me great Hope. This week prepares us for the the most horrible of deaths and the most beautiful of resurrections. He will Rise. But first He had to die.

I remember the week before Shannon's death. I tried to recall in detail each day leading up to it. Did I call her each day?

Did I speak words of love and encouragement to her? Did I assure her she would be alright? Did I give enough? Did I do enough? I know I did not answer all her questions. I know I did not stay with her the night before her death. I know I did not wipe all her tears because I am not God and I could not change what was to be.

That is really what Faith is all about, isn't it? Rely on God for everything. Knowing that He has all the answers, and I don't need to have them, because I trust in Him.

When I think of what Mary, Jesus' Mother must have suffered; it brings me to my knees. I weep for her pain. Seeing your Son, beaten, tormented and hung on a cross and left to die. And that took three long horrendous hours. What questions went through her mind? How did she contain her anger, her mother's love and the pain of seeing her Son die on a cross had to torment her beyond whatever a human could take? How did she do it? FAITH. And constant PRAYER.

Her example gives me strength and courage. This Holy Week is about what leads up to Jesus' death and new life, the new life that My Shanny is now part of in Heaven. God is awesome!

I miss my Easter Angel, but know she is sharing this Easter with Our Father. I hope He likes "Peeps"!

Thursday, April 5, 2012

Just a Dream

I woke up startled. I almost picked up the phone to call Shannon. Then, I remembered I couldn't reach her...she really is gone. It came so fast- her face, her lovely, sweet, smiling face...it was right there. So close, I could touch her. Feel her silky hair, smell her fresh soapy scent. She really was right there. I threw open my arms and waited for her to run into them. She simply disappeared. Dreams can be cruel.

I have been anxious all day. I can't seem to get my mind where it should be. I stare at her in the pictures on my desk at work. It seems so real, her being here. She should be sending me an email soon asking me how my day is going. Or calling me and putting me on hold, because she really is too busy to talk, but we like to hear each other's voice throughout the day. Or wanting to know what we are doing this Sunday-it's Easter. Where's a good hunt, Mom? Let's get all the kids and take them on a good egg hunt, right? We can do that Saturday in between ball and scouts, and shopping and laundry and gardening and whatever else she had on her agenda, but we would fit it in!

I am somehow shaking my fist at the sky and giving God a piece of my mind about life's unfairness. My tears are running down my face, my nose is running, I am stomping my feet and raging at Him about missing my daughter...when all of a sudden it hits me...He needs me right now. He is so sad right now. He is hurting, too. His Son is about to be beaten and crucified for my sin. Then He will hang on a cross to die for my salvation. Not only does the Father know this-He had to ask His Son to give His life for us. He felt the love of a Father and the fear and the pain of the Son, for me.

Now, He cradles my baby in those same loving arms. And He fills my heart with His love and that of my grandchildren. He knows my needs and He completes my story. He fulfills my dreams.

Tonight He blessed me with the sweet hugs of Olivia, my youngest grandchild and time with Shanny's three. JD

(Shanny's oldest son) answered the door and hid behind it, blew a whistle and I nearly jumped three feet off the floor! He thought that was hilarious. His smile and giggle was Shanny! Not in a dream-right there for me to hug! God does provide. Little Gus had me laughing with his humorous take on a video game...he is so not 4 years old. And Eva, she is my wild child. She has Shannon's love of life, her free spirit, her natural ability to believe that she can do anything she sets her mind to...dance, sing, entertain...we had a grand time while dad was out.

Before I knew it, dad was home, Evie was fast asleep on the couch, Gus was curled up in his chair with momma's blankie, and JD was finishing his computer game for the evening. Me? I was feeling less anxious, more loved, and so very grateful for a God who knows me so very well. He gives me what I needed and it wasn't just a dream-His love is for real!

Saturday, April 7, 2012

Easter Promise

It is through this Easter holiday that I truly have hope.

Through the Risen Christ I will see my daughter again! This is a

promise that I will claim-to hold my angel again...How do I thank

God for that gift? That promise of love fulfilled by His only

Son's death on a cross...for me, and if you choose-for you. There

are no strings attached to this gift-purely His love eternal.

So while I grieve for the loss of my daughter while I occupy

this world-her face, her sweet smile, the beat of her young 34 year

old heart, the sound of her laugh and her warm hug. I know that

someday, I will see her and hear her laugh, and touch her

face...again. Glory be to God for His Easter Promise.

For those of us who have suffered the loss of a loved one,

we know the pain of the empty chair at the holiday table, the side

of the bed that does not move in the night, and the phone that

does not ring. We know the terror forgetting for even a moment, what our loved one was wearing on that last day, the last words we spoke, or the last words we heard them speak.

We also know the guilt of smiling for the first time after they pass, and laughing out loud...again. We know the comfort of the numbness and the loneliness of the darkness. We remember the way our heart would stop when we thought we saw them on the street, only to realize it really wasn't them...it couldn't be them.

But through this pain, through this trial and this journey of fear and unknown searching, we hold strong to our faith, we hold unto Him. We rest in Him, for He is Life Eternal.

He is My Hope.

He gave me His Easter Promise-

Blessings to everyone who walks with me on this journey, I can't tell you how the power of prayer and faith has taken me from the numbness to recognizing God's love, even in the sadness and the grief. He brings me opportunities to share love and joy, to honor and to praise Him. When our minds are filled with His goodness, it leaves little time for anything else.

May the Blessings of Easter be yours and May your Hearts be filled with His Love.

Thursday, April 12, 2012

I Am Hurting

The past few days I have been sad. Since Easter I really know, Jesus has risen and I am truly blessed. But I can't stop my heart from hurting. When people asked me how my Easter was, it was very difficult not to burst into tears this year. I miss Shanny so much my stomach hurts. I know it will pass and I will cope again, but right now, today-I am hurting.

For no apparent reason, my eyes will fill with tears and I will want to cry. I will catch a scent in the air that will remind me of Shanny and I will want her near. I find myself hugging my pillow during the night and waking up more frequently. I feel that heaviness in my heart that I cannot fill. I want to cry a lot. I don't want to talk very much and I am feeling lonely even in a room full of people. I just miss my baby.

I received a message from a young friend today. She was requesting prayer. You see she lost her husband about three years ago. She has three young children and this Friday would have been her wedding anniversary. My heart aches for her. I prayed for peace and serenity for her spirit. And I prayed that God would heal her heart. I asked God to help me reach out to others in pain and to look past my own. God opened my eyes and my heart to a new level of understanding through that email. That young woman is a mother and a widow raising 3 small children. Her faith astounds me. She knows God's healing and the power of prayer. How amazing she is to recognize her need for prayer and to reach out for special prayer for Friday. She didn't ask for a selfish reason...she wanted to be able to recognize the blessings she had while she was with her husband. How beautiful! No self-pity, no anger or bitterness. I immediately prayed and will hold her in prayer again and again. She is a beautiful young woman and I am proud to call her "friend."

God has richly blessed me on my journey by continually giving me people who hold me up and who teach me the power of prayer and to hold strong to my faith, even when my heart is hurting. Even when I want to hold Shanny and I know I can't. And when I am reminded I am not the only one who grieves for the loss of a loved one, He gives me the opportunity to reach beyond my hurt, and to help someone else in pain. Because when I pray for someone else, when I think of someone else, when I reach out to someone else-I am not dwelling on myself. It is healing for me to work through my grief by helping others. Whether it is babysitting, running to the store for someone, picking up their dry cleaning, or running another errand-stepping outside my grief, gives me comfort.

And so for now, I will pray: Thank you Lord for knowing my needs so well. You are here to wipe my tears and to help me wipe the tears of others. You show me how healing it is to listen to others and to reach out and touch someone else in need, whether it is for prayer or service or just to talk. You made my heart, Lord, and you know when it is weak with worry or hurt or sadness. You know how to soothe my soul with Your guidance and your patience and your encouragement. I want to be like You, Lord. Please make me an instrument of Your peace. I want to be a child always in amazement of Your Wisdom, Love, and Mercy. Thank you for Your love and gentle touch. Thank you for healing my wounded heart, for filling that emptiness and for cradling me, Father. Please give me the heart of a child and the innocent unconditional faith to let go and Let God!

Saturday, April 14, 2012

I Am Trying

I am struggling still with sadness. Missing Shanny has kept me in a funk for a while now. Usually I can pull myself out of it after a bit, but lately, it has been very emotional. It seems to be affecting most everything I do.

I am not energetic as of late. I do not have the energy to do the things I need to do, much less should do, or even have the intention of doing. "Wanting to do" isn't even on the list. I can't muster up the mojo to get a move on!

My heart is so heavy. The sadness is overwhelming. Everything reminds me of Shanny and makes me miss her even more. I am saddened when I think about her, and sad when I don't.

Things are out of whack. My eating habits have gone awry-junk food is my friend now and I don't eat much in the way of normal food. I sleep for a couple of hours and then wake up for several more. I can't seem to stay on task for periods of time without losing track of what I am trying to accomplish.

My mind seems like it is unfocused, confused. I might be doing it on purpose, to try and block the hurting. I don't know, I only know I miss Shanny and even praying isn't helping right now.

I know there are dark days even with faith, but they drain me. Physically, emotionally and spiritually-these days take a lot out of me. I want to cry out and I can't. Tears aren't always the answer. The intense pain just won't stop. The physical pain is deep inside my heart. I can't seem to reach it. I am exhausted. I keep a prayer calendar for others. When someone messages me for prayers, I put them on my prayer list. If they mention a special date, I note it so I won't forget to pray especially hard for them on that date. This seems to help a little because it takes my mind off me...and my pain. It forces me to realize I am not alone on this journey of grief. It isn't all about me. So, get off the pity pot, Rose!

I read emails from others, their stories, their lives...what they are going through. It hits home. They are just as lonely, just as hurt, just as sad. I am not in a private club. All of us are members and don't want to be. Missing our loved one hurts.

Time, they say-heals. I admit, the pain is different from last year. It is not as immobilizing. I function somewhat better now. I can work and even hold a conversation to some degree before my mind drifts. I take less medicine, less often to cope with the anxiety and the pain.

Most days I smile. You would say I have generally returned to normal, whatever that may be. Not today, not yesterday or the day before. But this struggle is for me to figure out. I give it to God and I take it back. He will let me; after all, it is my struggle. He certainly doesn't demand I give it to Him.

I have left it at His feet, walked away...and actually gone back for it. I can't let go. I feel like a traitor when I let go. I keep telling myself-I am not forgetting my baby, I am just trying to live in this world without her in it. Believe me, it is not easy. Somehow, that does not feel right. As her mother, I don't feel I have the right to be here, and her not. I should have gone first; she has three babies and a husband-who need her desperately. I think that is at the root of all this sadness. My grandchildren want their mommy. My son-in-law wants his wife. I am a poor fill-in for her. I am not her. I cannot fix this. I am powerless over this.

So, I am reaching out and asking you all to pray that I have the strength and courage to give it to God. One more time-Let me, let Him heal my wounded heart so that He might use me to reach out and help someone else. That is really what I am doing here. I am here to love and serve. Please Lord, help me be a good servant, and reach beyond my pain and grief and show your face to others so that they may see Your power and Your strength and Your gentleness and Your awesomeness. You are the Great Healer of sorrows, Lord. I am blessed to know your love and your mercy. In Your Sons most precious name...

God Hears Me

When I pray-God listens. He hears my plea. My sadness and tears are not ignored. That is the beauty and power of prayer and faith. I have spoken with many of you, and emailed some of you recently, about the power of prayer. I know it seems like right now-the place you are in, this pit of darkness; the hole you cannot climb out of-there is no end to the pain. I have been there. I truly know your pain.

I promise you-Give it to the Lord, and He will provide for you a path. It might not be the same as mine. I pray every day for God's presence and continued strength as I walk along His chosen path. This is a journey of hope-of faith. I gave my life to Jesus and said, you have my daughter, now prepare me. Do whatever you need to with me, so that I might someday see my daughter again.

I have much to do along the way and I ask God to give me the opportunity every day to encourage others as He and the Holy Spirit have enriched my life in the midst of my grief and pain. I cannot explain the transformation, nor would I try. I simply believe. I know the Lord-and He keeps His promises. I cannot quote the bible verse for verse, but this much I can tell you-He is real, His power is real, He heals and He cares. I could not have made it through this past year without Him. He is my strength. He listens when no one else does.

The family and friends may get tired of hearing me speak of Shannon and how much I miss her. But He doesn't. He never judges me in my journey; He only supports me on my life walk to the Gate of Heaven. I fall and He picks me up. I stumble and He wipes my scraped knees. He whispers in my ear-Do not give up, Child-I am here. Come closer, I am here for you, lean on me; I will always be here for you. If you just ask for me, I am there, reach out and I will take your hand. He lifts me up when I cannot stand alone. This is what He has done for me and will do for you. Be open to

Him. Listen with your heart for Him to speak to you. Soon, you will feel His comfort and peace.

When I ask My Father for Peace He grants it in different ways. Sometimes, He gives me rest in the form of sleep-true bodily sleep. Other times, when I am sad, He brings me laughter through my daughters, a conversation with them, a memory that we chuckle over or they call me about something one of the grand kids did at school. Sometimes, when I really need comfort, the greatest blessings come from my grandchildren. They give me the purest kind of love. It is so real and unplanned-it just happens! I see their Momma's in their eyes and their actions and that makes my heart happy!

God does know every hair on our head, every thought in our mind, every word we speak before we speak it. What an awesome God we serve! How blessed are we that He hears us when we pray?

Thank you, Jesus for listening with YOUR heart! Thank you for Your unconditional love, that is never ending. So, if you are feeling that sadness in the pit of your stomach-give it to God.

Let Him wrap you in His arms and comfort you. He will. I will pray for you if you contact me through my email or blog. I will pray and God will listen because God Hears Me...

Saturday, April 21, 2012

Feelings...

I know they are there. I just can't describe them. You know what I mean? I can't label them. I am not any one thing: sad, angry, frustrated, I am all those emotions today.

Tomorrow is Eva's (Shannon's little girl) First Holy Communion, one of the bigger events in this little girl's life. Not only is Shanny not here to see it, but Eva didn't have her mom here to go with her and pick out her white dress and bride veil, her white patent leather shoes and lacy socks and it just isn't the same when a Grandma does it.

So, I am trying to get through the emotions and talk with God about what I am feeling so I can really enjoy the day and be in the moment. I am trying to converse with God one-on-one about it. My sadness and anger, I am saddened because Shannon would have been so proud for tomorrow. This is such a big day in Eva's life. Moments a mom wants to share with her daughter and a daughter wants to share with her mom: Mom rolling your hair the night before; Hanging your dress up with the slip, crisp and white; the new shoes still in the box and the fancy socks laying next to them so that fresh out of the tub or showery; our clothes are ready to put on for your special day. Downstairs, mom is preparing the food for the get-together after Mass, the house smells clean, and the cake has been ordered with the First Communion Figurine on top...wait a minute-that is my memory...maybe it wouldn't have been that way at all, even if Shanny were here. I can't say what it would have been like in the Dodson household. I can only tell you I will miss my daughter...

I am sorry for my selfishness; I think I am frustrated with myself for feeling this way. I think what should matter most is that the day is wonderful for Eva. That is what Shanny would want more than anything. So, I am trying to set aside my grief for the day, to reach past this sadness, even if I have to pray minute to minute to get through it, I will. Shannon would have been rushing around like a mad woman to make this day special for Evie...dress, cake and party...Nothing would have been on time, ready or planned, that was Shanny...and yet-it would have been perfect. Somehow, Shanny made it that way; the way a mother can and does...I miss you daughter; I am remembering your special touch, your sweet, special touch today. I will reach past my sadness and missing you and join in the festivities...

I love you, Shanny.

xoxox

All the way to Heaven

Mom

Right to My Heart

Whenever I am with my grand babies I see Shanny. I hear her in their voices when we play hide and seek and I see her in Evie when she dances and sings...our version of American Idol. Little Jason jumps out from behind the door, it never gets old, he giggles-it's his mamma's laughter I hear, I can see her throwing her head back to laugh, Jason does it the same way she did. My breath gets caught in my throat when I see him do it. For one tiny moment it takes me back to a different time when my baby was here. All too quickly, I realize my memory has fooled me once again. Right to my heart, I can't explain the feeling...it isn't pain, it isn't sadness, it is an emptiness of sorts, a void, that will never be the same again.

When I am talking about her, there is a point in the story that I reach every time, when I stop-because I am remembering her, the way she was, alive and happy, silly and giggly. She wasn't always that way, but that is how I like to remember her. When I get to that sweet part of the story, the part that goes right to my heart, I stop for just a moment, hold her in my heart, and then go on with the sharing of the memory...that is how it is now.

When I go through a picture album or CD with Shanny moments, it can be healing, but also difficult. It makes me long to hold her, to feel her heart beat, to hear her breathe and hear her voice. I try to remember all of those, and when I can't recall them, it goes right to my heart. I begin to panic. Am I beginning to forget? No, I am just tired today. Tomorrow will be better. I remind myself, some days are better than others.

While I am writing this post, I read several emails and other posts from people who have lost loved ones recently. One lost a husband, another grandparent, yet another young child, and a boyfriend.

Today, a mother lost her 23 year old daughter to a hit and run driver. Now, she must get to know the world of grief of a child. I would never want anyone to have to know this pain and heartache. I prayed especially hard for her today. I remember the fog God envelops us in a barrier against the pain. at first. I don't think I could have processed nor stood the physical pain of hearing the words at that moment that I had lost my daughter. And I now know God knew and was prepared long before I was. He was holding me up and keeping me sane through that devastation. Because He knew it would go right to my heart.

God has it under control-even the most horrible of situations we face-the death of our child. He knows the walk we face, the journey that challenges us and the spiritual fuel we need to get through it. If we turn it over to Him, He does provide. I have given it to Him several times on this journey, and taken it back. For some reason I want to own my grief at times. And then, I can let go of it again.

For now, I will pray for all those who have lost a loved one recently, especially a child...please Lord keep Your hand upon them. Keep them close to You; and keep their loved one closer. Our children are the air we breathe and the steps we take...I know because all of my Angels go...

Right to My Heart!

How Far is It To Heaven

Lord,

How far is it to Heaven? I just want to know so when I dream I make sure I can fly far enough in my rocket or on my carpet to see my daughter...I miss her.

Lord,

I only need one wish, not three. Please.

Why is 'if' such a little word with such a HUGE meaning?

Lord,

I know you are listening, so if I close my eyes and picture my baby, and then open my eyes...will she be here? Just sayin'.

Since you are God, will you make it Feb. 9, 2011 again? We'll call it a 'do-over.'

Lord,

I know they have visiting hours in hospitals, can you make a schedule for visiting hours in heaven?

Do you know the song, "Stairway to Heaven?" .Can you tell me where those steps are located?

Do you know who this Jack is with the magic beans? I need to grow one really tall beanstalk...

I miss my daughter so very much some days; I make up silly sayings like these to keep me from totally losing it. It helps keep the gloom and doom from getting overwhelming. I get sad and it doesn't always come out sad to people I love. It comes out grouchy or angry sometimes. I might be snappy to a salesperson, or not too friendly to the grocery cart guy. Usually, I am a very caring individual, but when I get into a sad place I have a difficult time recognizing it for what it is. I don't smile as much and I don't feel 'right' with the world around me. I have learned to do whatever works for me to get me through those times.

Today, I have chosen to write silly sayings. Another day, I might sing a made up song. Sometimes I journal my thoughts, and some days I have a good old fashioned cry.

There are days when reminiscing feels wonderful. I can see her smile and feel her presence. I am at peace with God's will, other days not so much. No matter what I do or how hard I try, I am in tears and nothing that day is going to make me feel better. On those days, the only thing I can do is pray.

Through the pain and the tears and even the anger, God listens to my words of love, of anger and confusion. He hears my pleas for peace and understanding. He knows my heart's desire is to do His will but the struggle is human-I miss my child, His child, too. He truly understands. So, He consoles me and comforts me. He listens with His heart to all my fears, my thoughts and all my questions.

Even, the silliest of questions..

Father, how far is it to Heaven?

And He smiles.

Friday, May 4, 2012

I Will See Her Every Sunday!

I see her in the flowers...

I see her in their smiles...

I will breathe in her scent with the blooms of spring and watch as

her love blossoms for us to gather up...And when the rain falls, I

will know it is her tears watering the roses of the garden. When the

sun shines once again, I will feel her warmth and know her spirit is

with us...Just as this beautiful flowering bush will root and grow...

So, will my knowledge that my child rests with Our Heavenly Father...As the weeks turn into months and the seasons change and pass, this will not change-only the strength of the flower to withstand the winter's cold and winds that arise and the storms that come...

The buds may close and sleep, take rest in the earth during this time, but when the Lord lifts the clouds, and raises the sun again, so will flowers burst forth their beautiful blooms.

When the Lord warms the days and sets the birds in song ...we will know her beauty again and again, forever and always...just like the roses that bloom year after year...Shannon, too will greet us with her beautiful sweet memories...

My heart is so full tonight with gratitude for the beautiful folks at St. Luke's for this wonderful tribute to Shannon. I will see her every Sunday now, when I go to church...

Saturday, May 5, 2012

Good Grief!

I believe today with the sun shining and the warmth

creeping into my bones, this will be a good day. I will try to do

something good for someone else today, so that my grief will seem

further away, at least for a time. I will reach out if I need to, my

family and friends love me, they understand my need to remember,

to talk, to visit Shanny, if only in memories...I will pray. I call it

having a conversation with God, because I don't repeat

memorized prayers so much as I talk with Him, and I try to listen

with my heart when He speaks to me.I will take a walk today. I will

breathe in her scent in the flowers of Spring and see her in the

butterflies and hummingbirds. I will listen to the sounds of nature

today. They can calm my wounded heart and nourish my soul. A

God that can provide such beautiful music knows my heart and my

needs, and He does provide. I will listen to the song of the birds,

as they sing to one another and pour out their love song.

If I am strong enough today, I will sing my song... I make them up. I may not be able to sing on key, but God hears my joyful noise and He smiles. And if the rain comes later in the day, I will take refuge from the storm, or dance in the rain. I like to march in the puddles and make a big splash!

God does not ask us to mourn without a glad heart. I believe He wants us to recognize His goodness far surpasses what this world has to offer. I believe He wants me to Trust in Him and know that with her last breath in life on earth, He was already holding her hand and welcoming her into Heaven as she took her first breath of eternal life.

These are my beliefs and they calm my hurting heart. They console and heal me when the pain still comes and the sleeplessness awakens me to the reality, she is not of this world any longer. When that pain takes my breath away, I pray for grace. Grace, to accept His will, not understanding, I will never understand tragedy while I am of this life, but I can pray for acceptance and grace to reach beyond my pain and do something good for someone else. Because in doing good, it hurts less.

There is beauty in the day that God has made. Embrace it, live it, share it!

I know my Shanny would not want me to be sad just to be sad, because I thought that was expected. Grief is different for everyone. Sadness takes on its own form. It morphs into many different shapes. But Shanny would want me to greet the day and make the most of it, love her children, don't let them forget their mommy, and she would say...

"Good Grief, Mom...get up and get moving...it's a beautiful day, don't waste it!"

To honor her memory, I am trying to experience 'good grief'...

Love you, Shanny-hugs and kisses all the way to heaven!

Mom

Sunday, May 6, 2012

Out of Nowhere...

The day dawned sunny and bright. Cheerful thoughts when my eyes first opened and my feet hit the floor. Thankful for the new day, cup of coffee in hand, I was computer bound to pay some bills and get some bills together to mail and make a bank run...normal Saturday stuff.

Pet the dog, feed the cat; second cup of coffee; read my emails; remember to let the dog back in; and refill her water bowl...I am on a roll.   Litter box-cleaned - check.

Dog food bowl filled - check.

Dog inside out of the heat - check.

Cat, where is the cat?

Under my chair - check.

Last minute check, bills in hand-ready to go, out the door-forgot to kiss the hubby, back for a second, kiss, kiss-check. Out the door, off to the bank, radio on-memory sneaks up-out of nowhere-tears, sobs, gut-wrenching bawling, can't breathe, stomach hurting-miss my daughter pain. Out of nowhere...

I don't know what happened between the car starting, radio on...and the racking tears. I can't really tell you how or why-it just is what it is, when it is, what it is, and that is just how it is...some days. Those tears must have been locked inside me, stored up. I didn't feel like I was saving them up, but some days I can't figure out what, why or when...looking back on it. Does it really matter? I just had a moment, that's all. I should be able to cry when I have to, wail and shake my fists at the god of the unthinkable beast called "death" that stole my daughter from me...The thing is, I am not angry, not at My God, anyway. He is a Healer of the Heart and a Protector of the Soul...He is making sure Shanny is at peace in Heaven..

That is something I really want to know. I have read that when people go to Heaven, they no longer miss this world. They would not want to come back...Part of me gets that and part of me says-did you know Shannon? She lived for her husband and kids. Part of my grief process was coming to terms with not being able to ease my child's pain any longer. I had no way to console Shanny. One moment she is kissing us and smiling her smile and saying...see you in an hour, fully expecting to see us, her husband and kids and go on with life...and then----no more smiles or giggles or outrageous comments.

Only did I see my baby under a white sheet, a little saliva still on her sweet lip. I remember dabbing at it and thinking, this cannot be real...in a moment someone will tell me you are asleep and will be awake soon...but that never happened. And so, I stroked her silky blond hair, kissed her many times, held her hand and wept for what would never be...

Over a year later, I am still weeping and am sure I will be for years, maybe until I leave this world. The pain is always the same-in my heart, where no one can reach it. No doctor can fix it. No medicine can cure it. So, I will pray. The words today are in my head, but God hears them. He listens with His heart. So when we have a heart-to-heart, it makes a lot of sense...the words mingle with the tears and I ask for grace and acceptance of His will, always. Thy Will Be Done, Father. But I need strength to cope, grace to accept and Your love to spill over...Help me, I am weak

and sad and broken, but with Your touch I will be greater than my

pain. Amen

Do Angels Cry?

When it rains the Angels are crying...I have heard that since I was a little girl. You know, like when it thunders, the Angels are bowling... Now, that saying matters to me-I want to know if my Angel is crying. My daughter Shanny, does she get sad, does she mourn her life with her family here on earth? Does she miss my hugs the way I miss hers?

And where do we get the answers to these questions? Who in this life can tell me about my daughter in Heaven? I couldn't sleep again and was missing her so, Mother's Day right around the corner, my birthday, too. I'm sure I am reacting to all of this, but I am saddened by HER loss. I feel she was robbed of her joy way too early in her life. She absolutely loved her kids beyond reason. She had her days, not all were picture-book perfect, but she was a terrific mom who knew how to love. What she didn't get right the first time, she was willing to apologize for and try again...

I know I am afraid the kids will not remember her. That saddens me to think they don't remember the hugs and kisses and peek-a-boo, and car rides, and vacations, and dinner times and birthdays and Christmas Mornings, and a million other memories they should have with their mom they will never have now.

I think I am angry. I have never felt this way before and I might be experiencing anger with the situation itself. I know I am praying daily not to hate the reason for her death, and I ask God to give me the grace to be forgiving because it is not my job to judge others. But, I am her mother. She was mine, to birth, to raise, to love, to nurture and to watch grow in her family life, and in the end...she was mine to bury. Please pray with me for strength to go through this part of grief. I do believe this is the worst.

I remember when my girls were young. Taking them to the doctor even for a checkup could be trouble. If it meant shots, I either had to turn my head or leave the room. The thought of anyone-hurting my children, turned me into a raging crazy person!

If I thought a teacher was too rough on them or unfair-many trips to school later, one of us left with a better understanding.

Shannon was your classic "good girl." She was easy to raise and not difficult or moody as a little girl. She spent a lot of time with her MiMi, her grandma and grew extremely close to her. She could melt your heart and win you over with her smile and personality. As a teen, she became more of a challenge. Even then, she had a way that seemed to be out of her era. She was a free spirit, more of a 60's product of life, than an early 90's teenager. She was never really wild or out to make trouble. The hardest thing for me was her smart mouth and her decision to move in with her father for a while.

Following that time period she attended college and had a strong positive attitude and frame of mind. She dated some but not outrageously, and when she met Jason-that was pretty much where her love story was written. It was not a simply written story either. There were many chapters that I thought would bring it to an end but always, the two of them managed to resurrect it and eventually they worked through all the issues and built a beautiful relationship and a strong wonderful marriage. Their three beautiful children are the stars of their love story and it should have lasted much, much longer. So many chapters were left unwritten.

But I am not the critic of life in this world. I don't get to orchestrate or plan lives out. I am only human and have to watch them unfold as God would allow them, regardless of human error by doctors and tragic mishaps that cost my baby her young 34 year old healthy heart to stop beating-forever.

So, if I sound angry or upset-I am. I want to know if my Angel is crying in Heaven. I want to know if she is missing her babies as they grow up each day without her. I wonder if she misses their kisses and their hugs. The countless-I love you, Mom...from morning till night that was music to her ears and the chatter and laughter that filled the house daily. I wonder if she is saddened by the thought that she will never see them graduate from schools, go to their proms, date or get married. For Shanny, college was a huge part of life-so, watching her children graduate was always in the plans and now she won't be a part of that either.

There are so many events those kids won't have their mama there for and so many events that over the past year she has already missed, birthdays, holidays, First Communion, backyard parties, her own 35th birthday party. I don't get it, Lord. Why when there are so many bad people in this world, did she have to go? Why?

I am struggling with my anger and my faith and the desire to see my daughter again. I am sad and angry and hurt and broken, Lord. I don't want this pain. I do not want to question Your plan or Your will. I don't need to understand, but I do need to accept. I cannot do that without Your grace.

Please, Father God, grant me peace and acceptance of Your will. That is my prayer for today, for acceptance of Your will... Because today, I am sad and angry and I want to know if my Angel is crying...In the end I couldn't wipe away her last falling tear, I couldn't take her hand and make it better. I couldn't do the things a mother is supposed to do when her baby cries...and I am saddened by that thought-that her last tear fell on her pillow and I wasn't there to wipe it and kiss her brow...so, Father, please kiss my Angel for me. And if she is crying, wipe away her tears, and replace them with Your Heavenly love...

Please tell her I love her...that I will always love her. I will never forget her and I will keep her memory alive. I see her in the children's faces, in their eyes. I hear her giggle sometimes and I see her dance moves when Eva is rocking out! Her love is all around and lives in each one of her children. She taught them well. How to love, how to give, and how to live...her words...

I want to live

I want to live

I want to live...

You are, Shanny, in your children and through them, you shall forever be remembered and live. So, please do not be sad, and please don't cry, my Angel.

He Heard My Prayer

I pray for acceptance, always. Acceptance of His will. It's the only way I can get from one day to the next. Prayer is so very powerful. It is truly a conversation with God. Whether it is a joyful talk, whispers late at night or sobbing into my pillow, He listens. When I am ranting at Him with balled up fists, angry at the loss of my daughter and the unfairness of it all, He listens. When I am gulping for air because I can't stop the flow of tears and I can't talk through the sobbing, He listens. When I am at peace, and praising Him for His mercy, He listens. When I want answers, and the silence overwhelms me, He listens. When nighttime comes and the quiet deafens me, He listens. When I pace the floors and ramble on, He listens. When I sing for joy but don't know the words, He listens. When I pray for others, He listens.

How do I know? I feel peace in my heart today. He put it there. He heard my prayer and knew I was struggling and brought me the gift of peace. My life changes every day and how I accept those changes is up to me. I know I must have God's hand on me at all times, and so I pray. It's my choice, I know.

My birthday was special because the voices of my children greeted me early in the morning with wishes for a happy birthday. My grand-angels sang to me and that put a smile on my face and my son (in-law) sent me a picture of my daughter and me together on an outing...it was so special; it is now my profile picture on FB.

Of course, my sweet husband greeted me with coffee and a smile and the greatest of hugs, ever. Friends sent cards and called, I received lots and lots of wonderful birthday wishes! That evening I got together with my sisters and my brother for a great cake and coffee gathering at my sister's house. I even got to visit with a few of my nieces and nephews. It was a beautiful day filled with a lot of love and many blessings. I felt Shanny's presence through the love of my family and friends holding me up. I felt her love shining through. I felt her smile as I blew out my birthday candles on my cake and I felt her giggle at the number of candles on my cake...gosh, mom, that could cause a fire! It's getting hot in here...

All because He heard my prayer: He listens to my heart as it pours out to Him every need. Even when I question why? Even in the midst of anger and pain. Even in the darkest of hours...He hears my prayer. I am never alone, for He is with me always.

Even when I don't hear His voice,

He is listening to me.

When I don't feel the answers are coming fast enough,

He is listening.

He hears me always; I am sometimes talking so loudly I can't hear Him... Sometimes, He is quiet and I just need to relax and let God be God, and rest in the knowledge that He heard my prayer.

Monday, May 14, 2012

Mother's Day 2012

A Conversation With God

Today is Mother's Day. I prayed for all Moms everywhere. Especially my mom in Heaven and Shanny who is in Heaven instead of rushing around the house brushing Eva's hair for church and getting Gus to go potty before leaving the house for church...this is where she should be...but she isn't.

And I know, I should be more accepting of God's will and trusting Him and my faith should lead me on my journey as I go through the necessary steps of grief to finally accept the death of my daughter. But, sometimes it just isn't that easy. Sometimes, on days like this, it actually is quite difficult. When I look around church and see all the little families with the mommy and daddy and kids and then there is Jason and the kids and me...

I question God, why? I know you ask-you just posted that God heard your prayers and gave your peace, and I am here to tell you that was yesterday-today is today. My grand babies are here, with flowers in hand, and no mom to give them to...so yes, I am a little upset. My human-ness does not like my grandchildren hurting. I don't like seeing my son-in-law trying desperately to figure out how he can be both mother and dad to his kids, because today is Mother's Day and the kids have no Mother, not in this world, not in this life, not in this church, not to go home to, ...he is dealing with his own world of hurt and I can't fix it for him, as much as I want to. My heart aches for him. God spoke to my heart today. God said-plain as day-trust me-if you love me-trust me.

I said-God, if you love me, help me. Help me accept your will, and help my children accept your will without hurting. I want what is best for my grandchildren. I made a promise to Shanny and I want to keep it. It's Mother's Day and I want to be a good mother, is that so much to ask? How can I be sure the kids will remember her? How do I know they will remember how very much she loved each one of them? Who will remind them every day when they get older? Who will tell those stories and point to her picture and ask who this is?

Shanny's greatest fear was that the kids would forget her, and I promised her two things...one, that I would always keep her memory alive for them and two, I would always be there for Jason and the kids. Neither one is a hard promise to make or want to keep.

God said-Do you think I want any less for your Shanny than you do? Do you think I want any less for Jason and the children than you do? Do you think I want your girls to hurt and miss their sister so terribly and that I don't care if they are hurting?

I was quiet. For once, I did not have an answer. I am 'mom' but He is God...He created me and my Shanny and Jason and the children and my children and Mother's Day...so, yes, He gets it. Does that make my pain any less real? No, of course not, but I do need to consider when I pray, the words I am saying...Our Father, who art in Heaven...Holy is Your Name. This is one of the only written prayers I actually recite...it has such deep meaning to me. It brings me to tears and very often, to my knees.

On this very special day of days, I want to remember Mary-Jesus' Mother-who knew my pain so well. She knew the pain of giving her child to God, watching Him suffer horribly and hang on a cross, and suffer degradation for hours before He mercifully died. Did she feel anger, I wonder? Did she question God's will ever? Did she cry out, God stop this-You are all-powerful, don't let this happen to my son. Because, her faith was so strong, I don't know. I know the love for my girls, but I am not sure if I cannot question God because I am human. But I do know this-God understands. He knows my questions, my anger, my fears, my sadness and my pain. He hurts with me, and weeps with me, and soothes me when I break, because His love for me is greater than my pain or my sadness, or my anger or my fear.

My Mother's Day was wonderful, with my girls and grandchildren filling my heart with love, my sons (in-law), I rarely include the in-law...loving them like my own, and my husband, my sweet husband, understanding my need to be busy...I got to spend time with my sisters, since it was Joyce's birthday on Saturday; we spent time together twice this week. Yes, it has been a week of blessings. So, in my sadness and my anger, I remember to pray, because God is good and He is bigger than my pain. And today is Mother's Day, and I am thankful for my beautiful mother and the Blessed Mother who knows my pain and shares my tears, as well as my joy.

Happy Mother's Day today, tomorrow and every day to all the mothers that have gone before me, and the mothers that are in this world now caring for their children and loving their way through it all... As my mother used to say to me, May God Bless you and keep you close to His Heart.

Wednesday, May 16, 2012

That Beautiful Face

This is Shanny and Her Three Angels...

When I woke up, Jas (Shannon's husband) had posted this on FB...I love that man. He does the most thoughtful, wonderful things. Shannon told me moons ago, many things about Jason.

Some of which I will share, others–I will not. She said...He is a man of honor, a man of respect. He loves his family. He loves his work and the people he works with–they are important to him. He cares-deeply. He has character and morals. And he is gosh darn cute! She really didn't have to sell me on him–I was hooked!

Back to this picture...This is my girl with three reasons she smiles, JD, Eva and Gussie. Aren't they beautiful? I could always feel their energy as a family, and still do when we are in church, but it saddens me that some of that energy is missing...it was created by their love for one another. It was the summation of a whole...the definition of 'family.'

She is one of three reasons I smile. She created in me a desire to learn, a willingness to try new things. Whether it was food, traveling or clothing styles, haircuts, color and fashion not always her strong suit–but I went along with her a lot! Her humor was contagious. I should re-define this by saying, Shannon often had my hair different colors–once she convinced me she could frost my hair, it was no big deal. I believed her...for days I looked like a dingy yellow striped skunk from the neck up! She thought it was hilarious, but I had to go to work like that until I could get it professionally corrected. I allowed her to wax my lip, my chin and my eyebrows. She would giggle and I would yelp. I was a bit hairless and she was entertained for a while...

We had some really good times. Some of those times, we really didn't talk about anything of great significance, we just spent time together. It would have been running errands with the kids, shopping for any one of the many unnecessary items we both loved, or hanging at the house puttering around.

She knew how to make life look easy. No matter what she was up to or struggling with at the moment. Shannon could smile through the most difficult of situations for the most part. I would often call her for technical advice on the computer. I could hear her silently laughing as she instructed me through my traumatic episode.

Sometimes, we pushed each other's buttons. There were days when a phone call might not go as we expected. Once of us might say something and the other took it the wrong way. A day or so would go by and one of us would call and that would be the end of it pretty much.

Look at that beautiful face. It says so much about her. Her beautiful spirit, her love as a mother is shining in this photo. You can feel the pride she has in her family. Truly, this was her life and love...She seemed happiest when she was busy with Jas in the kitchen, out in the yard, or hanging out as a family. That's what made Shanny beautiful from the inside out. Jason and the kids completed her beauty from the outside in...

She accomplished much in her young 34 years and taught so much more about life than I could ever dream of...I truly was her student. She had her faults, I know but I don't need to dwell on them, they are unimportant now, just as they were when she was alive. I try to overlook every one's faults now, because really, life is too short to get stuck on the little stuff that really doesn't matter.

I like thinking about the stuff that make for good memories...the stuff that was full of smiles and laughs and kisses and hugs, and a few tears...sounds like a Hallmark card? Well, maybe, but I'll take it! I sure do miss that beautiful face but I'm sure that is what God said for 34 years until He called her home...I bet

when He saw her again He greeted her with...

'Sure did miss that beautiful face, welcome home!'

Sunday, May 20, 2012

Testing, Testing...Can You Hear Me Now?!?

I am blessed. I know it. And yet, I am angry. Why? I keep asking God the same questions so I am wondering if He can hear me. It has been over a year since My Shanny was taken from me. Not just me, but her entire family: her husband, her children, her sisters and MiMi. So many people are hurting, and yet there are no answers. I know, I know-hence the title of this blog, right?

My daughter told me she was worried about me, I was isolating. I am lashing out at people that don't deserve my anger. This isn't their pain, it isn't their hurt, and it certainly isn't their fault. To them, I need to apologize...I am misdirecting my hurting heart. She is right; of course...I am doing that. It is ironic, lately we have changed roles. I was the one who was holding her up and trying to guide her through her grief and show her the power of prayer and faith...

I had a friend who recently said she was also concerned. She couldn't imagine my pain, but Shanny is at peace now and would want me to move on, to be happy because she is happy. Part of me wanted to hug her and at the same time, part of me wanted to snap at her...I AM WEAK! I AM STRUGGLING!! I DON'T KNOW IF I WANT TO BELIEVE.and before the words came out of my mouth I knew I had to pray for courage. I want to accept God's will in all things. I really do. But some things are not easy to accept. Time is said to be a healer. In matters of the heart, I am not sure if that is true. I miss my Shanny, the same today as I did when she was taken from me. It is no easier now. I am just coping a little better because time has passed.

I think there might be testiness to my prayer lately. There is more of a cranky, hurting tone in my prayer. I have asked for peace, I was given peace for a time. I have asked for patience, I had that for a time, as well. I continue to pray, but it is getting more difficult, as time passes to be accepting of other people's reactions. I do not like it when others move on through life as if

Shanny was just a fleeting moment in their life...I believe she should be the center of every conversation, all the time-so no one forgets just how special and wonderful and beautiful and amazing Shanny made this world!

I know that is probably not a realistic approach-but it is my reality for now. I do not like hearing, she is happy now, so move on. I do not like change and I do not like it that I do not have my daughter to hug or kiss or talk with or be mad at or laugh with, or argue with or cry with or any of the things we used to do when she was here with me..

I do not want to see her kids without their mom. I do not want to see Jason without Shanny at his side. I do not like seeing her headstone in the cemetery and no matter how many flowers you decorate it with, it still means the same thing. She is not physically here with us anymore. Well, I don't like it one bit! Can you hear me now, God? I am angry and I want to know why You had to have Shanny! When there were so many more reasons NOT to take her, You took her. I just don't get it! I have read,

"When God Doesn't Make Sense", and the real answer is You don't have to answer us.

You don't have to give us any answers at all-that is where my faith comes into the equation. I can't really say that comforted me, but I do know I believe. After all the ranting and raving, I do know this to be true-My God does hear me. He loves me and He understands my anger and my anxiety and my pain. I will continue to pray and I will continue to believe. And I will probably have days when I will be angry and sad. I will shake my fist at God and yell;" Can you hear me now?" And He will answer me with love and patience, because it won't be the first time and it probably won't be the last...

Tuesday, May 22, 2012

Thank You for Sharing

Today was a better day. Better than what? Better than the days when I don't want to get out of bed or can't seem to pull it together. Better than the days when crying seems to be the only response I am capable of that day. Better than wanting to scream for the pain to stop hurting so I can get some much needed sleep.

I had the opportunity to see my son (in law) graduate on Sunday from STLCC. I sat next to his mom and saw in her eyes the pride and joy she had earned as his mother through the years from the days of where he has been to what has brought him to this day. I loved seeing the joy on her face and the unshed tears of childhood memories mixed with the excitement of the day and seeing one of your dreams come true. It really was beautiful.

His mom shared some pretty powerful words with me that day-look back-look up and move forward. That seemed very fitting for a graduate and it could really apply to everyone in any life situation. I am not ready yet to move forward, I am still visiting my past and constantly looking up. I look up so often, I trip over my own feet! But, they are great words-thank you for sharing!

One of my sisters shared some moments with me and allowed me to feel what I needed to feel-anger, frustration, sadness, and to know it was okay. God would understand, He loves me and wants me to go to Him, to give it to Him-anger and all. But I need to learn to let myself feel-and not be afraid to share my inner feeling with God, He already knows them, but He wants me to trust Him enough to go to Him. Really good food for thought: thank you for sharing.

Sometimes, when I read an email my instinct is to fire one right back without thinking it through. I don't always allow myself to digest what the email really says. I don't let myself feel the contents, I just read it. I learned from a really good friend-if it is worth reading, then it is worth taking the time to read it thoroughly for its true meaning, no matter if it is a book, email or a letter...Again, really good advice-well worth sharing!

No one said this grieving process had a specific outline. There is no checklist to follow. I have to experience my own grief and own it. As much as I wanted to believe I would not go through anger, I am going to have to travel that road. I don't have to take up residence there, but I have to recognize it, and deal with it or I will never move past the anger. Maybe, I am a little frightened of the intensity at times. I don't want to totally let go or I am afraid of what monster will surface in me. I have always been a "Mama Bear" when it came to my kids; I can't imagine truly confronting this anger head on.

I will continue to pray on it and ask for God's grace and guidance as I navigate through the anger phase. I don't even like the term-anger phase. It seems like I am minimizing the grieving process by compartmentalizing my emotions. I know grief is a process, but truly-it feels like I live here now, so why not get used to it.

Thank you to all my friends who read and share this story and journey with me. Your comments and thoughts mean more to me than you could know. Just the fact that you value me in some way to trust me enough to share your stories and your own journey with me brings my heart such fullness. We really do not have to take this walk alone. Our journey is our own—but we can hold each other up—in prayer and in sharing moments of encouragement and love. So, while I will continue to take my journey in faith and lean on the power of prayer, thank you for sharing!

I am really missing Shanny today. I talked with Kim and Tina (my other 2 Angels) and they are having it a little rough also...so I decided to post some pics of our Girl to brighten our day...

Sisters...and a couple hubbies, too!

My Three Angels, the Day Kim got married-these are some serious smiles. What a wonderful day we shared...

Our Snuggle-bunny doin' what she always did best...her favorite blanket, reserved for precious few and only on an as-needed basis!

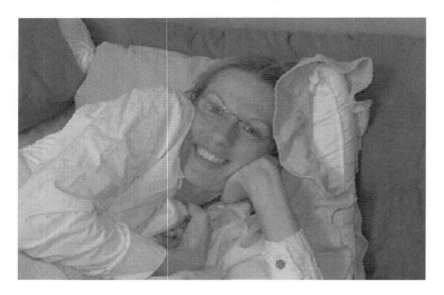

Shannon's smile could always light up a room, just like her spirit lights up the sky now!

Shanny has that "movie star" quality. She made life look so easy and fun. No matter what she was doing or where she was going—you could bet she was going to have a good time!

Look at those smiles!

Wedding Day-August 2009. I Had Never Seen Her Smile So

Beautifully, or more full of beauty...

Saturday, May 26, 2012

Am a Work In Progress

What a crazy, wonderful, sad, memorable, eye-opening, week! Love pours in when the prayer pours out. Did you ever wonder how God so keenly touches each and every heart at the moment it needs touching with the exact touch it needed by the person whose touch you were craving? Even if you weren't aware of it!?!

That happened this week a lot...I haven't been getting the best rest, but I was sleeping. I have been agitated to say the least. People have been getting on my nerves more easily and I noticed myself snapping and over-analyzing comments and even FB posts. Really, I was tempted to shut down for a minute because I was feeling too many emotions. The pure and simple facts are I miss my daughter Shanny. I am working my way through this grief process one day at a time. Frankly, no two days are ever alike and most every day is not the same as the day before. One day I am feeling the presence of God strongly-He has me firmly in His grip and is not letting go. I am strong and I am making progress, and then the very next day not so much.

Now, don't get me wrong-God still has me in His grip-it is me who is letting go, and I know it in my heart. Some days my head and my heart are not in sync. It is like there is a total disconnect. Does my faith change-NO! But I am human and I stumble. I get sweaty palms and my hand slips away for a moment, but I know God is waiting for me...He never takes His eyes off me. But He allows me to find my way back. Because the lessons I learn along the way back, are what keep me moving in this life. Those lessons-moments and words of love, random acts of kindness, sheer and open emotion shared with a co-worker, an unexpected hug from the grocery clerk.

All these moments, these lessons in love and life are the energy I need, the juices that make my heart pump joy and the very reason I CAN and DO reach for God's hand again. I call it His Spirit in Flesh. He allows me these beautiful blessings and encouragements and then I in turn am so filled with His love and the Spirit's gifts that I want to share my joy. That's on a good day!

Not every day is like that for me and I am sure not for you either. The only difference is–I am struggling with the acceptance of my daughter's death. You might be struggling with whatever it is you are working on in your life. The name for my struggle is grief.

The emails I read every day tell me I am not alone, they tell me of love that is shared between mothers and their children. They tell me of the joy in hearts that have been crushed and stolen and robbed and taken for what seems like-no reason. I cannot tell you I understand. I do not. What I do know is I am weakened by my loss, but I know God and He can overcome any loss, any pain, and He will take your hand and your heart if you allow Him. He will and through the power of prayer, your faith will begin to soar. So, if you have even the strength to give Him just enough faith, tiny as it might be. He will take it and grow it stronger each day. Will He give you the answer that we all want right now? WHY? Maybe He hasn't revealed that to me, and I do not even ask anymore. Instead, I pray for acceptance of His will, and strength, to pray more for those that cannot pray for themselves, because their pain is too great right now. I ask every day that He allow me to reach at least one heart with a word of hope.

I am a work in progress. I cannot begin to know your pain-it is just that-YOUR pain. But I can express my caring heart-because that is what I have to offer, a caring heart, a listening ear, and a tender shoulder. Blessings on this holiday weekend, prayers for our soldiers and their families, and all the Veterans who have gone before them; and hugs to Heaven for all of our Angels!

PS-To Kim and Tina, my Angels here, I love you more than you know and hope your journey is one of peace and understanding. Give it to God and do not take it back...He will see us through our pain, because He is greater than any sorrow and more powerful than death...

There is no shame in any struggle that helps us grow. There are no tears the Lord cannot dry and there is no greater love than God's love for us. And then-He created Mothers-to love and nurture and nourish their blessings, their children. So, it stands to reason that when our blessings are called back to their Heavenly Father and are no longer here with us-our hearts will ache and sometimes, break. It doesn't mean God no longer loves us-because He calls them home to heaven. Rather, I believe-His love is so great and His belief in us so strong-that He is rewarding them with Heaven. And to us, their mother's-isn't this really the greatest gift we could pray for and have answered? To know our child is resting in the arms of their Heavenly Father? In a Heaven where there is no pain, no illness, no sadness, no darkness-only beauty and light. Heaven is a place where they can sing their song and dance and laugh and play. Even if they could not do those things here in this imperfect place-I believe in Heaven they can do all things.

And so I pray that one day I too will go home to Heaven. To hold my dear daughter in my arms again., to hug her and kiss her with the love that only her mother can give her, because God chose me for that most precious duty. Until then, I am His and I pray for His love and mercy and the guidance of His Holy Spirit every day while I take this necessary journey through grief. Like I said, I am His and I am a work in progress...

Blessings!

I have spent the last few days lazily taking turns between my hammock and the bench in the yard. Holidays can be a good way to reflect on what is really important in my life. First of all, never having been in the military, I owe a great deal of gratitude to those that serve my country and their families. Without them, I wouldn't be enjoying my freedom and the lazy days in the hammock...

Secondly, I feast my eyes on the blessings of the Lord. My family-God has richly blessed me with a loving circle of loved ones that reaches far beyond my dreams. I am married to a wonderful man with a great family; my children have grown into beautiful, strong women with families of their own. They have blessed me with 8 Little Angels that make me smile from the inside out! And beautiful caring friends-who know me and still love me!

There is just one flaw in this magical picture. My First Angel is not with me to enjoy the fruits of our family. She was called from this earth last year and I am learning to say it, read it, live out and accept it every day. I pray a lot for strength and courage to face the painful realization of her death. I ask the Holy Spirit for grace and mercy to accept the Father's will, because God says to pray to His Spirit for help...Some days, I just want to close my eyes and remember when...

I was a little girl with no worries or deep thoughts.

The most important thing on my mind was playing Four Square or Red Rover.

When I could sing out loud in church and no one cared if it was off key-

God loves joyful noise!

Having my best friend on a Florida trip was the best summer ever!

High School was the biggest challenge I had to face.

Dating was actually fun...

Driving wasn't expected, it was a privilege.

Graduating high school really meant something special..

College wasn't a given, it was earned.

Working your way through life was the norm.

Settling down didn't always mean as a married woman.

Having my First Baby was one of the most important and happy moments in my life!

Feeling unconditional love from my daughter-was the very best life had to offer!

Finding my way to Jesus was a troubled journey with a lot of falls.

Angels #2 and #3 came along-life was magical because my children were and are magical!

Marriage didn't always work out but you didn't have to hate to end it.

Taking a trip to Wal-Mart could be an adventure.

First haircuts didn't always turn out as planned.

School recitals were powerful and prideful!

Watching my girls grow up meant accepting we might not always agree on things..

I could fix a lot of hurts with hugs, kisses and ice cream.

I felt like I was the most important person in the world to my three Angels...

I held them on my lap-and they were no longer babies.

Wiping away a tear was just the beginning of feeling my heart strings tugged...

Knowing the right answer wasn't always what mattered most-sometimes it was about listening.

Getting a phone call meant something good was going to happen.

Not having a lot of money really didn't matter.

School clothes shopping never ends...

Watching them cross a stage brought tears to my eyes and shouts of praise...

Wedding plans are a lot like shopping adventures-only more expensive.

Seeing them in their wedding dress-priceless!

Being in the room when they have their first child-takes your breath away...

Hearing the news, another one on the way-brings smiles and tears and lots of jokes...

Holding your grandchild I suddenly remembered holding my

Angel for the first time...

How all three have such different personalities-I loved that about

them.

Saying 'no' really meant 'no.'

Staying up late was something special-not because I can't sleep.

I made a promise to my mom and wanted to keep it-because it

mattered to her.

There are so many remember when memories-I can't name them all

and some I want to steal away in my heart forever.

This I know-when my girls say remember when? I want them to

smile and remember when remembering was a blessing...a shared

memory-a moment in time that will forever be on their hearts. A gift

of time shared-that no one can take away or changes, because I

remember when...

I wonder if you can see us walk through the door of life...

It happens every day, when I am with Jas and the kiddos; I am so loving my moments of joy and hoping snapshots are going to heaven.

When life hands me a child's smile, I feel blessed and hope I had something to do with the reason for the smile.

When I see Jas relax-even just a little-I hope I can bring him some comfort, because he fills my heart with love.

When I hear Gus' laughter-it brings me such gladness, and hope that he might be joyful again. I know he will miss the touch of his mother who can never be replaced. Those hugs and kisses must come from heaven now and find a way right to his heart.

Eva's dance and energy remind me of you-Eva tries to make me laugh and succeeds! She is teaching me to let the 'happy' in-I find strength in her approach to life-the same approach you had-Look out World I Have Arrived!

J-Bug has a gentle heart but is letting the sun in slowly, as if he is savoring each ray and only shares the sunrise and sunset when he feels safe. A beautiful spirit, but you knew that...

I see Jas with the kids and my heart leaps for joy as he is mastering his life-one day at a time. The love he shares with the kids, I hope you see it because it would warm you inside out and outside in-he is an amazing father and example of living life, love first!

Your sisters are rising up and holding onto your spirit-Kim has grown in self-confidence and is moving forward-family first, you touched her life more than you ever knew and taught her about family...

Tina promised she would go back to school, and she is...16 books, classes with names I can't pronounce and a determination that you showed her and courage she didn't know she had, your encouragement to do what you want to do and yes, you can-outlook on life-keeps her going.

All these moments have been near to me for a long time-I just wasn't allowing myself to see them. Your beautiful spirit was alive when you were here with us-and it continues to breathe through your children and the memories you created for each of us.

The photos remind me of you; the memories create a never-ending story of your life and love for your family. I hope you see the snapshots in heaven-of a smile, a moment when all is good with the world, and you know we wait in joyful hope to complete our family album...

Tuesday, June 5, 2012

Grief or Depression?

Since I lost Shanny I have dealt with sadness beyond my
own imagination. I could always tell the difference though, between
sadness/grief and depression. Lately, I am experiencing difficulty
distinguishing between the two emotions.

Some days I can reflect on the past and it will not
emotionally hurt me. Lately it seems the sadness can overwhelm me
and I will unexpectedly fall apart. In my conversations and emails
with a lot of you we share some deep, painful gut-wrenching
sadness. I know that is grief-it feels like heart pain and not head
pain. Does that make sense to anyone?

At times like this I reach out to others who have shared this
same pain-loss of a loved one, a child, spouse or significant other
for reassurance that I am not losing my very weary mind. Prayer-my
strong daily companion and strength does not seem to calm my
senses or ease the distress.

That for me is so totally different than my normal. I am a little concerned, frightened even. I know sadness, I know grief, and I have been depressed before. I really don't want to spiral into depression because it is so destructive. Please say a prayer that I get a handle on this frame of mind quickly.

Stress, sometimes plays a role in depression also. Unwarranted stress-self-evoked stress, imagined scenarios that play over in my mind-they don't have a place there and they aren't real, nonetheless, these pictured events can cause havoc in day to day life. I wonder if it isn't better to just confront the situation head-on and get whatever it is out in the open and deal with it.

I applied for a promotion at work and thought I really had a reasonable chance at getting it. I worked on my resume, studied the questions before the interview, had a good feeling about the interview and felt pretty confident overall. I was devastated when they went outside the department to hire someone for the job. I let it eat at me for days before I finally faced my disappointment and frustration about it.

What it boils down to is this. I am a 57 year old woman looking at another 8-10 years in the workforce and I am a little frightened about the future for me...there, I said it out loud.

I do not always think straight. As a matter of fact-some days, I do not want to think at all. I find refuge in my work but I cannot always concentrate as well as I should. That scares me. I miss my Shanny. No matter how grounded I am in my faith, I am human...I feel pain and sometimes the pain is so great-it takes my breath away. I want my daughter here-with me, in this world...I can't help it-selfish as it may be-I am angry some days that God took her from me.

Prayer is a great expression of feeling. I can sob through an Our Father-but mostly I just talk to God-or scream at Him, or beg Him-for peace and understanding, because some days-it all eludes me. I do know one thing He never changes-His love for me. No matter what-He loves me. In the midst of my screaming and stomping and challenging His decision to take her-He will envelop me in His arms and hold me to Him. He will whisper-"Do what you must do-to get through this, I am here with you-give it to Me, "I will not let you go and I will never let you down."

So, in the middle of grief-can I become depressed? I imagine so. I must admit-I do not like the feeling of not knowing the difference. Grief seems comfortable to me now. Depression-I do not want to go there. Please pray for me as I will continue to pray for all of you.

...Because I know the Power of Prayer and Faith as a Mother Grieves...

My Role

Life has us in so many different roles at times. You wake up one day and you are a little girl getting dressed for school. You wake up another day, many days later-and you are getting your daughter ready for school! And then, if you are really blessed-you will wake up many days later, with grandchildren running off to school. This is supposed to be the normal cycle of life. Then, a wrench is thrown in the mix and your cycle is broken.

I have been very blessed, don't get me wrong. I have seen my school days, and I saw my daughter get on the school bus. I have eight beautiful grandchildren who are in various stages of elementary school and pre-school life. But, one blessing in my life that is missing is my daughter-Shanny. As life goes on around me, I can't help but wonder why she isn't here to see her son run the bases at his ballgame or see Evie dance like crazy or watch Gus play sword with a tree limb twice his size. This is not natural to me and it is hard for me to take much less adjust to daily.

Yes, it's been over a year. That's no magic passage of time for adjusting to a death of a loved one. I have learned there is no special date when it all falls into place and you just feel better about it. Actually, I am grieving more this year than I did last year. I am feeling more pain now than last year because I am capable of feeling the pain now. I am not wrapped in a cocoon of shock or walking in a fog like existence to keep me from losing my mind. Believe me, some days I wish I could go back there. It seemed easier when I was less aware of what was going on around me. I didn't have to cope with changes on top of changes. Life evolves and it is up to us individually to create a place we feel safe-to carve out an existence we can cope with in the end.

I have lived a good number of years before God decided to call Shanny home. But, she hadn't. That is the part I am questioning. Why couldn't He have called me? I am not as spiritual, true. I am not as holy or "good." I will give you that-I am not, but I am, one thing-I am in a better place to leave my grown children than she was to leave her three babies. That is the part that makes me angry and confused. Do any of you who have lost a child feel that way? Did you ask God why? I feel like I had many chances to get it right and if I didn't, then it was my own damn fault and if I hadn't gotten it right by now, chances are I wasn't going to get it right. But Shannon didn't really have that much time. She was just coming into her own, when God took her. I just don't understand it and some days-the darkness rules my mind and I cannot realize my role in this life any more. I can't desire to figure it out. I am exhausted from the heartache and the pain and the grief.

Can you understand? When it hurts to think about living without her so much the pain reaches deep inside me and seems to settle in my bones and body like a weight that can't be lifted. Some days it makes breathing a chore. My stomach aches and I become so ill I want to vomit at the thought of facing one more day without her in it. When the reality of her death creates pain it makes me want to scream out loud until I can't hear my own voice any more. It feels good to say these things out loud now. These are feelings I haven't worked through and need to face.

I try very hard to be a support system for my other girls. I want them to come to me and I want to be there for them. I also want to be there for my son-in-law. What I have to face is he might not want me to be there for him. His ties to me ended when Shannon passed away.

The common link is the grandchildren and I have no right or reason to expect more. No matter what I thought our bond might have been-our grief has taken us on different paths and our journey is our own. I cannot feel his pain nor can he feel mine. I need to come to terms with that and I will in time. I pray he finds peace and comfort in his life. I know he is doing the best he can for himself and the children.

I do not want to hear someone tell me-move on, move forward, look up, she is happy now, she is at peace..I know, I know, I know. But I am hurting! I cannot explain how angry it makes me feel when someone tells me she is at peace now. I have news for you-she was at peace before-she loved life. She loved her family. Yes, it could be tough some days, but she loved working at it and making it work!

So, frankly, I do not want to hear all the verbiage about heaven and peace and blah, blah, blah...I get tired of hearing myself say it. I am a believer-I know God and I know He gets it, but I am angry and I own my anger. I don't like this one bit. I do not like visiting her grave-I do not like seeing her sisters cry and weep with guilt because they thought they had time to work through their sisterly issues and now they have to live with their guilt because they didn't have time to repair old wounds. I do not like to see Shanny's kids growing up without their mom to do the things all moms do.

It angers me, it saddens me, it frustrates me, it sickens me and it makes me want to pound my fist on the wall of heaven and yell and scream some more, but why? It won't change anything. It won't bring her back and it won't take away the pain.

So, what is my role now? What am I supposed to do? Pretend I do not hurt, that I don't feel the pain of a mother who has lost her child? It doesn't matter that she was grown. She was my baby. I carried her in my womb and gave birth to her 34 years ago and she was given to me by God to raise and care for and nurture and grow and love.

Did I screw up? Sure I did. I made some bad choices in life. I had some fall outs with her but I did the best I could, and I loved her with my whole heart and all I was capable of loving her with at the time. I made amends and I know she knew I loved her and I know she loved me. I watched her grow into a beautiful woman with a joyful heart and giving spirit. I could not have been a more proud mom.

She taught me more than I can say about being a good mother and a supportive wife to her husband. She saw her husband through eyes of true love and she persevered through a lot of tough times. She was a strong individual who would not give up or give in without a fight. She approached life and love the same way. God, I miss her...and so, I keep asking the same question—what is my role? I know the answer—it is not always an easy one.

I see it every day. My role is to reach past my pain and my anger. To reconnect with the God I know and love, and to share

His greatness with others; to count my blessings and realize His goodness; to work through my grief and take one day at a time.

To pray for strength and courage to continue on this journey of grief and to grow in my faith and my love for God the Father. And my greatest role is my greatest role is to believe-always, to believe always in the power of prayer and faith. Even-as a Mother grieves...

Sunday, June 10, 2012

Today is a New Day

Prayer refreshes my heart. It opens my mind and soothes

my soul. Prayer seems to decompress the icky feelings and push

forward the happy feelings. I don't know if any of that makes

sense to any of you, but I know it does to me. Basically-God has

it in control. When I remember to give it to Him, I can begin to

exhale slowly. It doesn't mean I feel better immediately, but it does

mean I am giving myself an opportunity to take an empty box and

fill it with some of my most painful memories or problems that are

troubling me, I can even take a bit of the grief and gently lay it in

the box if I choose to, close it up and hand it to God. He doesn't

throw it away without opening the box. He just has a better

system for filing than I do. He knows what needs to be kept and

what can be discarded because He can be more objective. That

is how I look at it and it helps me.

Today, I will take a deep breath and try to enjoy this day. I am putting some emotions "on hold" for now and will pick up where I left off if I choose to another day. Right now, I choose-this beautiful morning God has graced me with, to breathe in the beauty and the sunshine. A cup of coffee, my patio and hammock wait!

What I am beginning to understand is that every day does not have to be totally about Shannon and her passing. I am allowed to enjoy my two daughters and my grandchildren without guilt and anxiety. This life is so very short. I have a wonderfully understanding husband who supports me in my grief but does not like to see me dwell in the sorrow. He often says-Shannon made you laugh and gave you a lot of happy memories, think of those, not just the sadness of her not being here. Sometimes, I get angry and tell him he couldn't possibly understand-he is not a mother. He quietly replies, you are right, I am not-but I miss her, too and I know that pain. I just allow myself to remember how she made me smile and I feel better. Just try it...

And then, we will talk, sometimes for a long while about her...until I am relaxed and can let myself take hold of the present, until another day and I need to visit her memory again. He is (my husband) an extraordinary man who knows me well and loves me in spite of my many flaws. I am so grateful for his presence in my life. He knows how to make me smile even when I want to cry...

I see Shanny in the smiles of her children. I often see her in their actions. I catch myself watching them and all of a sudden they will do something and I swear it will be something she would have done to the T! It makes me want to laugh and cry at the same time. I imagine that can be very painful for Big Jason at times. It must be bittersweet moments that bring him such closeness only to be reminded she is forever just a memory. My heart hurts for him. But today I am not dwelling on the sadness. I am feeling her smiles and her beating heart. I am feeling her in the warmth of the sun and the burst of color in the flowers. She is all around me in the garden and as the birds sing, I hear her whisper her love. I know she is with me and surrounds me with her joyful spirit. I am thankful because the Lord has opened my heart today and I am letting the sunshine of her love fill me.

Thank you, Father for Your mercy and Your guidance when I need it most. On the cloudy nights when I cannot find my way through the fog and on the stormy nights when I cannot hear the angel's gentle song because of the thunder in my mind, when my heart cannot rest and my eyes cannot find sleep. Thank You for finding a place of quiet where only You are and all else fades away. Thank You for gently rocking me until I find solace in Your arms and allow myself to dream of a New Day...

Saturday, June 16, 2012

Blessings Come in Different Ways

I have to recognize blessings for what they are and when they come. God sends them unexpectedly...They come in many different forms and I don't always catch them...Simple and yet so very powerful-

The first time Olivia says a new word-and I get to hear it! J-Bug smiling from ear to ear-it feels so good. Selena, when she says "I love you so much, Grandma".

At work I hear from a doctor that I am doing a great job or a co-worker thanks me for helping them. I get an email from an office I have made contact with a response I have needed to complete a file...

There are so many ways God blesses me every day. Just the simple act of waking up next to my husband-who smiles and says-I love you...Or the phone call from my sister who tells me how special I am for no reason...The friend who calls just to say-hey, I miss you...My son-in-law who calls-just to talk...

A memory of Shanny crosses my mind and makes me laugh out loud!(It must have been a good one!) The daughter who calls to take me out for coffee-for no special occasion...

Grieving is a process. It is learning to live without someone you miss in your life every day. It takes time to go through every step of grief. During those various steps-I still experience all the beauty of everyday life with my family and friends I am capable of taking in.

God still gives me the pleasures of tiny miracles every day, the sunrise and the flowers of my garden, my grandchildren's hugs and Sister time with my family...I have to make myself emotionally available to accept the gifts of friendship offered me, the love of my family and the assistance from my co-workers. No, it is not always easy. Prayer makes it possible and Faith makes it happen!

I was at a meeting yesterday and was challenged with getting all seven members to participate by commenting on making a change within the VA system if it was within their means-within

12 minutes. The trick was I could not tell them I had only 12 minutes to get them all involved and invested in the meeting and to contribute an idea for change. The only prop I was given was a musical wand... This was handed to me on the spot, I hadn't time to come up with an idea so I went with the child in me and became the fairy godmother of wishes-in a 150 words or less-if you could change 1 thing at the VA, what would it be?

I flitted and flew to each person at the table and tempted each one with the wand and gradually each one participated with a n idea, and a positive one at that! They became animated and giggly as they became part of the game and I felt really good about meeting the challenge. The feedback was terrific and it worked out and started off the meeting on a positive note! That was a blessing for me. Some days I don't feel like I am contributing much at work. Maybe, I am a little down or quiet. I am sad some days or tired, because I didn't sleep the night before. Some days I am replaying the day I lost Shanny, and I cannot concentrate or stay focused. Positive feedback brings me back and helps me regroup. A real blessing!

When I really focus on my blessings-not my troubles; My happiness and not my grief, I become lighthearted and able to reach past myself and offer them a friendly 'hello' or a helping hand at work, a neighborly wave as I take my walk in the evening, another blessing-recognizing folks I surrounded with every day. These people matter to me and I need to make sure they know they do!

Sometimes, Olivia, my youngest grandchild will take my hand and place it on her heart and look at me. I know she does this with her mommy. It is comforting to feel her little heartbeat, but more so to see her eyes shining and little smile. When she hugs me, it takes the weight of the world off my shoulders.

I noticed that about my grandkids-they can cure most of my ailments-a dose of their love, dries my tears, warms my heart, calms me down, brings a smile and brings me life and energy. Their love is so very special to me. God has taught me about so much this past year-what is truly important in life, isn't money and a status job. It isn't acquiring 'things' by working so much you forget you have family. It's about living out loud and loving your family.

Sharing your time and your energy with them, and telling them how much you love them and how much they mean to you- often. Each one of my children is different and I want to recognize their unique character and personality. Each one of my 8 little blessings brings me joy-each for a different reasons, how blessed am I? God is Awesome! So, when I get down, and I do-I have to wait for the storm to pass-and the rainbow to appear, and some days, there may not be a rainbow after the storm-so, I color my own, with my blessings. You'd be amazed at how beautiful a rainbow can be when you are the artist!

The power of prayer is truly my stronghold in this journey of grief, and my faith-it grows stronger because God never lets me fall too far before He catches me...another blessing!

God bless all the Fathers on this Fathers' Day weekend- those that are present and those that have gone before us and are celebrating Heaven Style...

Sit Next to Me

Today is a special day. I felt Shanny's presence strongly today. I have prayed for a while now to feel her closeness, to comfort me. I miss her so much. God is an awesome God. In His time, He brings us where we need to be.

Last night I spent time with J-Bug, Evie and Gus. I had Olivia with me so Tina could study. What a group they made. Shannon would have been happy I think, to see the cousins playing together and MeeMaw crazy in the midst of it all! Between, TV shows, our own talent show by Eva-Diva and the Gustard, with a little help from LuLu, and then Pizza and video games, and more pirates and make-believe...it was a successful night of Mee Maw time! The kids always lift my spirits. They teach me what life is really all about-the important part anyway.

So, when I walked into church today, I had much to be thankful for this morning. There was calmness in me that I hadn't felt for a while, a peacefulness that came over me and quieted my spirit. I closed my eyes and began to commune with God. I praised Him for my family, for the Fathers of my grandchildren. All three of my sons-in-law are very special to me. They are all very wonderful fathers. I have a special relationship with each one-each relationship a little different, because each one of them is different. I truly love and respect each one of them and feel blessed to have them in my life.

Then, as mass began, I prayed for forgiveness for my down falls during the week. However, I may have let God down-and I am sure I did, I asked Him to forgive me and strengthen me in His likeness, to be a better servant and to rely on Him more and myself less. I asked Him to guide my every waking moment and to nourish me as I slept. I asked that He guide me in my faith and lead me only in His path. I so want to know only His word and His ways.

As I prayed, I began to feel lighthearted and joyful. I took the kids to Children's Liturgy and we made little wrapped flowers for Father's Day and thanked the fathers for their planting of seeds of faith in our lives. When we came back from liturgy, I watched as the kids rejoined their dad, and I noticed just how much they truly loved him. How they held his hands and snuggled in close to him. I watched as he stroked their heads and patted their hands, rubbed their backs and kissed their heads. I remember when Shannon was here-it was much the same-only they both shared those privileges. The kids loved them equally and divided their love between both of them-but they don't have that blessing any longer. Mommy isn't there to hold Gussie and rock him, or rub Eva's back and hold her hand. She isn't there to hug J-Bug or kiss his forehead.

So, when I felt Shanny's spirit, I patted the pew-sit next to me, I beckoned. I envisioned her where she always sat-next to me and the kids in the middle of her and Jason, her beautiful smile beaming. This was when she was happiest. When she had her whole family surrounding her and she was in God's House. Together, I felt we had quite a conversation. Let me see if I can recall it for you:

Me: Hi, Baby! How are you?

Shanny: Fine, Mom. It's beautiful here.

Me: I have wanted this for so long, sweetie. Just to know you are at peace and happy.

Shanny: Everyone is happy here, Mom. Grandma and Grandpa, Papa, Grandma Tillie, Bill...We are all very busy though. Heaven is a place of beauty beyond anything you can imagine, really. There is no pain and there is no sadness, ever only joyfulness. Oh, mom-look, aren't the kids precious? And Jas-he's so handsome. Isn't he just the best, mom? I told you he was a terrific dad!

And she leaned into me and rested her head on my shoulder, just like she used to do. She snuggled in and for a moment I did not want to move because I believed it was all so real...

Shannon: Mom, I really want to sit close to them, be near them, breathe them in and remember them all over again. They are so beautiful!

Me: Of course, Shanny-then, come, sit next to me so we can remember what it was like...

Shanny: Mom, you can always remember-I am only a thought away. God promised He will never let you forget. I asked Him. I love you, Mom and I promise I'll be back. Thank you for being there for Jas and the kiddos...I love seeing them with you. It's just like I always wanted it to be, Mom. MEEMAW, I love that name, aren't you glad I came up with it? Now, am I your favorite?

And, before I could give her my standard answer-Shanny, I have no favorites-I love all 3 of my Angels the same...she was off flitting around. I did get a wave and a kiss, though...at least that didn't change...

So, whether or not I was awake when this all happened, I do not know...and I do not especially care. All, I know is My Angel #1 came to visit and sat next to me...The Power of Prayer is amazing and faith, well faith is what keeps me smiling on my journey...God Bless!

Sunday, June 24, 2012

Praying Outside My Grief

Reaching out to others brings my grief into perspective some days. Yes, I miss my Shanny. Will that change? No. Do I know she is safe in the arms of her Heavenly Father and lives in Heaven? Yes.

Today, I learned a co-worker has pancreatic cancer. She has a husband and kids and grandchildren. Very close in age, I feel her pain...and fear. I prayed for her.

I spoke with a dear friend whose child is an addict, and she is worried he might be relapsing. While she is finding strength through Al-Anon, he is fighting the addiction and hasn't taken responsibility for his choices. As a mother, she often absorbs his anger as he strikes out in pain. I prayed for both of them today.

My daughter is studying in school a subject that took the life of her sister-just last year; it is very difficult and emotional for her at this time. Because she has the will and the determination, I am praying for her to overcome the obstacle this area is presenting. Kimmy, my middle angel-is stressed and needs relief, she is depressed and hasn't reached out for help. I am praying she sees the benefit of counseling or medical advice to meet her needs and give her peace.

Many of the moms I communicate with by email, have suffered loss and are trying to find their way-my prayer is they lean on the Holy Spirit to guide them more and themselves-less as they take this journey.

A co-worker has smoked for over 40 years and is now on oxygen. She has tried to quit smoking but is finding the habit overwhelming. I am praying for strength for her to fight this terrible habit that is robbing her of her health.

Another friend is chronically ill. She seems to fend off one illness after another. It is nothing life threatening, but she often lacks energy and the will to get healthy. I am praying for renewed energy.

So often, I see illness strike young children and I cannot understand it. I have to pray for them and for understanding. I do not understand God at these times. When there are so many evil people in the world who deserve to hurt and suffer (I am reminded here-that I am not to judge-lest I be judged.)

I want so much to reach outside my own grief because I know all I have to do is to listen to the news and I hear of another mother who lost a daughter senselessly, gunned down for no reason, on her front porch. Why? There is no need to ask why-there is only a need to pray, for the mother and her family to find peace and to recognize the face of God. Somehow, some way-let His light shines through their darkness.

I can only say when I do something-anything, small as it may be, a smile, a kind word because those are prayers as well, for another person...it lightens my burden of grief; for that moment in time, I am a vessel of joy for someone else-and that feels good. That is the Power of Prayer and Faith as this Mother Grieves!

Friday, June 29, 2012

Heaven Will Wait

I have been feeling very sad as of late. So sad, that I really wanted to go to sleep and sleep forever. But, I was forgetting some extremely important people in my life. My other two Angels, who love me, and need me here with them, and to love them and my grand-angels right now, so, heaven will have to wait.

I am so blessed to have daughters who talk with me and not at me. They are such a blessing. I learn so much from them. All three of them have taught me very valuable lessons over the years. I am very proud of the women and mothers they have all become.

Seeing my doctor on Friday helped, I am sure. She adjusted some medications and added a mood stabilizer for anxiety. But my real source of help came from God in the form of a conversation and a long hug from both of my girls on two different occasions. The Good Lord provides us with the best medicine!

So often I get caught up in the grief of missing Shanny, I forget the privilege of being a mom doesn't stop because God called one daughter home to Heaven. I have two Angels here with me who still need me. I have an opportunity to do with them, some of the important things I missed doing with Shanny.

As sad as that may be, I cannot let the sadness overcome my being "mom" to Kim and Tina. They deserve my love and attention, too. I also have eight beautiful grand-angels to shower with love and affection! My life changed on Feb. 10, 2011 and it will never be the same again; but I cannot stop living and life is not waiting for me to move forward. I know it sounds terrible but life is happening all around me and as much as I want to scream at the world to stop and recognize the loss of my daughter-there are hundreds and probably thousands of other moms and dads who are going through the same grief.

From the outside, we look the same. Most people do not know what is happening inside our minds and our hearts every day. And sadly, most will not care because they are not affected by our loss. But isn't that true of other people who are suffering?

We all carry our own burdens. We must all take our own ownership of our pain and sorrow. We can choose to live there, and get stuck-and probably not survive the journey, or we can visit and allow ourselves time to feel our loss, grieve when we need to and continue to live our daily lives as best we can while we sorely miss our loved ones. The choice is always ours to make. There are resources to help us. We have the ability to see a counselor, or find an open group that deals with grief, visit blogs like this and vent as often as you need or journal on your own. Grief is a process and I am learning it is not a one-size-fits-all.

For me, I am learning day by day, if I lean on God more-pray, ask, vent to Him and seek the help I need here from a counselor or my doctor, if it gets to be too much to handle-I am on the right track. That might not be the answer for someone else. Their journey may be different. That's ok, too. I can be supportive of their grief process, but I cannot direct their journey, God is my stronghold and I do not know who they lean on for comfort. Prayer is my vehicle of communication for the most part. Singing on a really good day, and crying when it's not so good.

God knows me-He knows my moods, my feelings, and my days ahead. He has this. He holds me in the palm of His hand- lovingly....So, for me, I will continue to pray because I know the Power of Prayer and Faith as a Mother Grieves.

Amen.

I Am Grateful

Today, I am grateful. I am grateful that God loves me. In spite of my flaws-He loves me. He created me in His likeness, and I have done everything I can in my life to break me, ruin me, spoil me, tear me, hurt me, and destroy me...and yet-here I am. In all my brokenness, here I am. He gently pieces me back together, mends my rips, glues my parts, and gives me warmth and light and love to grow again...

I am grateful God thinks I am important even when I don't. He can love me when I am not very lovable. He forgives my outlandish behavior and encourages me when I am at my weakest. He thinks I am special and unique and He gave me purpose. His patience gives me hope.

In the midst of my grief, He holds me and rocks me gently. He soothes my broken heart, and allows my tears to spill over and water my seeds of faith. He knows I am hurting and carefully tends to my wounds and lovingly reassures me my life will take shape once again. He encourages and reaches out but never forces or bullies me. He knows the importance of family and friends in my life. He surrounds me with love. I am required to accept and be open to the love, but He furnishes it. Again, He will not force it on me but it is there waiting for me when I am ready to accept its presence. Outside my pain there is a beautiful world of healing love. I only need to open my heart and accept it.

God provides. I will never stop loving Him for His mercy and His love. His patience amazes me daily. His message is clear, isn't it? He will never leave us, if we love Him and abide in Him. No matter what my grief may be like in the darkest of days, I know He is there to lift the cloud if I call to Him. I only need to remember His name-Father.

And so, today-I am grateful...He has brought me back again, from the dark. Thank you Heavenly Father. I called to you and you heard me. You know my heart is hurting. I miss my Shanny. You reminded me of many blessings this world has given me. Many smiles I have shared, many memories that will forever linger and many words that are not yet spoken. My days are not yet finished here, my job is not complete, and I have not earned the right to Heaven's door.

I am grateful You are my Father, My Savior and My Friend...I have many more memories to create with Kimberly and Tina and my eight beautiful grandchildren and my David. I have a beautiful family and friends that for whatever reason, love me. I am productive in my work and I love being in this world to praise Your Holy Name, Lord. I have much to be grateful for today and every day because I know the Power of Prayer and Faith as a Mother Grieves!

Monday, July 9, 2012

Every Heart Has a Story

Today I am asking you to share with others. I want you to share YOUR stories. I want to know how YOU remember YOUR loved ones...

PLEASE share your memories with others. Share with your family, friends, church members, and work-family, anyone who has a story of family, life, love and need. I will pray with you, cry with you, talk with you, and listen-together we can begin a journey of peace-finding. Prayer is powerful and can be felt by many and heard by God from these pages.

Share your story of family and love. Share a fond memory, a need or a request for prayer. God answers all prayers...and He knows our names by heart.

I truly believe if we come together in prayer, our healing will begin, because we will be reaching beyond our own pain. We will reach outside of ourselves, no matter for how long, no matter how difficult...to help someone else. That is what life is about, isn't it?

I do not know your faith, I do not know your name, but I do know pain. I know what it feels like to look up to the sky and ask God why? I know the feeling of wetness on my pillow and realizing I had been crying again...I do know the catch in my throat when someone asks- how many children do you have?...and I know the pain of knowing I will never hold my daughter, Shanny again-in this life. I know that pain. And yet, I have hope. Hope of another day, another life, another place where I will see her and hold her .She will recognize me, and our time apart will fade and our time together will be forever...you see, I have faith. Faith in a God who loves unconditionally and forgives with such grace and mercy, that my life for all its mistakes and errors-have been forgiven and forgotten by the Only One that matters-because He loves me...And He loves YOU!

This is the hope I want to share-the hope that matters. Hope that gives grief a meaning and a reason. Please, open your hearts and share your story-you may touch a heart that had no hope. You may breathe life into a weary body who wants to forget...you may give them reason to remember...

We are here for a purpose, reach out and be someone's purpose. If we all think about it-we know the Power of Prayer and Faith as a Mother Grieves...

Just to See Your Face

What I wouldn't do to see your face

-I'd gladly scale a wall,

I'd climb a tree; I'd climb a fence,

a building 100 feet tall...

I'd climb so high, into the sky

- I'd reach an ocean wide,

I'd swim all the way to a sandy beach,

and hike up a mountainside,

I'd look for you in the glens and glades,

I'd look where you might hide-

I'd swim that ocean of heartfelt tears,

right on out to you,

the tears I'd cry would fill the sea

-water of pure deep blue-

What I wouldn't do to see your face-your smile-your eyes-your

hair-

What I wouldn't do

to hug you close,

and kiss your brow, so fair.

Oh, daughter, sweet daughter-I miss you.

Oh daughter, sweet daughter-I love you.

Oh daughter, sweet daughter

-I'm sending my love-all the way,

every day- until I see you again.

Oh daughter, sweet daughter

...just to see you again.

Saturday, July 14, 2012

Thank You, Lord

Thank you, Lord for Sundays...

Watching J-Bug, Evie and Gus in church warms my heart.

Thank you, Lord for Mondays...

Having spent a beautiful Sunday with all 8 of my Blessings (my

Grandkids), my daughters and sons-in-law;

I have a lot of new memories to reflect on today!

Thank you, Lord for Tuesdays...

Work was crazy but productive and challenging!

Thank you, Lord for Wednesdays...

The sun was out and the breeze was in the air! I felt You in the

Summer day.

Thank you, Lord for Thursdays...

Spending time with my sister always brightens my day! Whether

we are together or on the phone chatting, it warms my heart to

remember and to share our daily lives with each other...

Thank you, Lord for Fridays...

My husband and I spent time just getting to know each other.

Yes, we still do that-talk about silly things and important things.

We share our day and our dreams.

Thank you, Lord for Saturdays...

Today was full of laughter and warm hugs and smiles! It was a

wonderful day filled with You, Lord. Thank You for Your

presence in my life. You give me strength and peace. Somehow,

You always know what I need-even when I don't!

Thank you, Lord for Sundays...

So much to be grateful for, Lord...

Family and friends and the blessing of faith. You make the world

come alive with sights and sounds of life and beauty. In the midst

of grief, You show me how to love again and to remember my

blessings are still with me-eight of them, my grandchildren. My

daughters, my husband, my sons-in-law, my sisters, my family, my

wonderful friends, my co-workers, my church family, my neighbors.

So much to be thankful for, Lord...

Yes, in the midst of sadness-You will bring the gift of a smile to a burdened heart. You are there to listen, to comfort and to strengthen me; and I am brought to my knees in grateful prayer, because I do know the power of prayer and faith as a mother grieves!

Thursday, July 19, 2012

It Happened Again

It happened again. A girl about your age turned around and I thought it was you. I know it couldn't have been, but for one brief second-I thought it was. This happens on an average of about 2-3 times a week. If I am lucky, I don't burst into tears when I realize it isn't you for the thousandth time...

I have seen you in church, in the supermarket, in the resale shop, in Kohl's, in the salon, in the post office, in the dollar store, in the mall, in the park, at the theater and at the library to name a few places. I have approached some of your doppelgangers and struck up a conversation, but that is disappointing in the end, because they could never be anything like you-only you were you.

Sometimes, I find myself telling the whole story of how you passed away to a total stranger to ease the pain, and for a few minutes it helps. The pressure seems less and the hurting subsides a little. The throbbing in my head goes away for a bit and I can breathe without gulping in air...yes, after a year and a half, I still have these days.

My therapist inquired recently-so, no matter how much time passes, you can't seem to get past this? Needless to say, I have a new therapist. Medicine dulls the pain, the symptoms can be treated, but the ache of the heart is real, and only God can heal that pain.

The reason I am writing today is for affirmation, I think. I need to know there are others who have experienced this feeling of seeing double, so to speak. Then, the total letdown of realizing the fact that my child still lays buried in a cemetery and God did not choose to raise her and bring her back to me.

...Okay, I'll admit it, I did pray for that in the beginning. I prayed first it was a nightmare, and I would wake up. Then, I prayed, God would bring her back to me, crazy as that seems. Then, I realized how selfish that would be. We are living our lives to prepare for eternity in Heaven and I was hoping to rob her of that residence as I am recounting this story to you...I did retract my prayer. God allows that you know. If we realize what we are praying for is not right-we can go to Him and say-I reconsidered, that would be unkind or selfish, please disregard that prayer, and He will. He knows our hearts, He just waits for us to know our heart and then He smiles.

I hope and pray for folks who are experiencing their own painful loss, that they too, find solace in the smile of our Heavenly Father because I know the power of prayer and faith as a mother grieves!

Sunday, July 22, 2012

The Most Amazing Thing Happened Today

Shanny,

Today is Sunday-Jas posted a picture of the kids at the beach. They look happy-for kids without their mom.

The beach looks pretty-for a beach without you on it-in your little suit and floppy hat. You always looked so graceful and sweet on the beach...just a couple of years ago, you were on that beach with your floppy hat.

That's what I can't grasp or understand: The 'why' of it all. What has your death accomplished? I know God understands my frustration. He doesn't flinch when I ask. My faith is intact, I just don't get it! You were so much to so many here. You were wife, mommy, daughter, sister, friend...so much...

I am trying to reach others who grieve, Shanny. It helps when we share our pain because we are not alone then. We can vent together, pray together, remember together, and some days, try to forget together...

Am I being selfish, Shanny? Because I miss you so much and I want you here with your family? Does that make me wrong? I believe in God's plan, I do; but my human-ness wants to hug you and kiss you and talk to you on the phone and email you at work, and laugh with you and cry with you and get mad at you and know you are still here with us...every day...to wake up to...that's what my heart says it wants. So, does that make me a bad person? So, I go to church with a friend today, right?

God knows what's on my heart. He knows the pain, the frustration. I did not plan on attending this service today. It just happened I had this Sunday open and I had been invited to attend this service before, so I called my friend and asked if I could tag along. This is like no service I have been to before. I mean that in a good way...the people gather in fellowship before service and visit and then hear the word of God and sing praise. The vocals are good and the Spirit is there if you want it.

Here is the key-they played a new song today...This is not my home...it speaks of earth and knowing we are only passing through, we are just preparing ourselves for Heaven...the pastor spoke of having lost a loved one too soon and feeling out of touch with the loss. That's me, I wanted to shout!

Who told him I was coming today? And then, I felt my Shanny...it is okay mom-I am home now. Heaven is my home. It will be your home someday, too, but not yet. You must finish your life on earth first. Only God can decide when you are ready to come home, mom. Please don't feel so sad-there is much you need to do in the world you are in while you are there. You cannot tell God His business. But you have to tend to yours. Mom, you have the girls and grandchildren and family and wonderful friends...they need you and love you.

You are here today because God knows your needs better than you can ever imagine and He knows your desires long before your heart ever feels them. Trust me, mom. When your time comes, it will be far more special than anything you could envision-ever. But, it is not for you to decide. Your job is to pray, to believe and be grateful for the blessings you receive and to trust in the word of the Lord-always in all ways!

And in all her Shanny-ness she had delivered the message she was sent to deliver and she was on her way! I had to smile to myself. Why? You ask...because if she were here, she would have done the very same thing.

Yes, I am so very blessed to know the power of prayer and faith as this mother grieves!

Monday, July 23, 2012

Good Morning, Angel!

Shanny,

How do I express to others the importance of your memory? I mean-here it is, almost your birthday again and I am running through my mind what to do. Some folks think it is crazy to celebrate your birthday, others just shrug their shoulders, and others just don't get it at all.

I know you aren't here to celebrate your birthday-I am not crazy, but I also know that day will always be special to me-it is the day God blessed me with my Angel #1! How can I not celebrate? Is it something I need to do privately? I am puzzled by people sometimes...when they say-if there is anything I can ever do, if you ever need to talk, don't think you are alone, I'm only a call away...blah,blah,blah...

Do I sound perturbed, upset, and pissed off? Well, I am! It is bad enough you're not here to celebrate your day, much less planning a birthday party for an Angel...that's it! That will be the theme! A Heavenly Birthday!

I see it all now...candles, feathers, white fluffy clouds...why are you giggling? What do you mean-am I crazy? I don't know-am I crazy? No, what do you mean no - Angel Food Cake??

Okay, then smarty-pants, you help me plan it. Together we can plan and have a grand celebration of your life on August 27th- I love you, Shanny...your new Angel friends are invited, too! What's that? No, I won't bake the cake-I promise...you just get the buzz out and spread the word-we need ideas!! Hugs-all the way to Heaven, daughter...because I know the power of prayer and faith as a mother grieves!

Yes, even in grief, we must learn to smile through the tears! We need laughter to ease the pain and everyone loves a party!

Wednesday, July 25, 2012

How Do I Know?

How do I know when I talk with you-that it is really you? I mean, is it me? Talking to me? Or is it you...Sometimes, I think I want it to be you so badly, that I sense your presence, but then, I wonder if I am making the whole thing up, because I miss you so much.

How will I know?? The thought of you close to me is such a great comfort to me. The conversations seem so very real. Even the voice inflexions-I can hear you saying the words I hear in my head...does that mean it is really you, or that I have a very vivid imagination that includes audio affects?

I pray and ask God but I am not sure if I am really listening for the answer...I want to, but I'm not sure I'm really ready for the...this is God speaking speech-the voice you hear is NOT Shanny's...I don't think I could handle it. Then, my next question is does it really matter if it is indeed Shanny? Is it enough that I believe it is? Is it hurting anyone if it isn't my sweet baby? All the comfort I get from our visits and our talks...I can't imagine why God or anyone would want to take that away from me.

So, why does it bug me so much? Why am I asking the question? I think I really want to know the truth. Someone asked me if I believe in mediums. I know it is considered evil in some religions. If anyone could tell me if there are any 'real' mediums, then maybe I would consider a reading. Right now, the only One that knows the future is God. He is the only one who can give me answers if He is inclined to do so.

I am not sure where this blog is headed, it is getting heavier than I intended when I began to write. But I do feel that many of us as we grieve for our loved ones encounter situations when we feel we might benefit from a reading or a psychic of some sort. I believe it has to do with the level of grief I am in at the time. How deeply I am grieving for my Shanny at the moment that predicts my weakness or feeling of inclination to delve into the psychic world.

My faith should always be in charge of my doubts. But there are days, like today, when I am missing her and I want to know she is near me. That is when I feel her–it really is her I am feeling. It is not a coincidence, not a fluke; it is really the essence of my daughter. I want to know that it is a real feeling and not just something I made up in my head. I want to know God blesses us with these feelings and encounters, and that I am not imagining her closeness out of loneliness for her. I don't want to deceive myself...

And so I will pray for more insight–or faith, or understanding or whatever God says I need right now at this very moment. God knows my heart. He knows my needs and He knows my faith and my desire is to please and grow in closeness to Him... Because He knows that I know...

The Power of Prayer and Faith as a Mother Grieves!

Friday, July 27, 2012

Forever 34

I just realized that when I look at your last pictures, you will always be Forever 34...

You didn't even get to celebrate your 35th birthday with us, we celebrated alone.

I don't know what made me think of all this at 1:50 in the morning, but...yes, I do,

I was looking through my photo album and thought; I need some new pictures of you...

When I realized "new" pictures to me, would be earlier pictures of you from Jason...

And the cycle of pain, raw pain begins... I can't help but feel robbed of your very life and presence. A mother is supposed to have her children long into her old age, to love and comfort and share stories and memories of days gone by. So, I am not the only one robbed of your life-Jason and the kids, Kimmy and Tina-we all feel the loss so very deeply and sadness overwhelms all as we move through this life without you.

Mine is different, I know. I carry the pain of all three of my children. I cannot fix or take away your sister's pain, and I can't ease Jason's. I helplessly watch J-Bug, Evie and Gus grow up without their mom and the anger sets in... Damn the doctors and damn the senselessness of it all! It isn't fair, and just it isn't right...I want someone to pay for destroying my family. I want someone to feel the pain of what one moment in time has done to the rest of my life. I fight and I struggle every day to move forward in this journey-this walk of learning a new normal-beginning a new reality-a life without you in it. WHY!?! While others go happily about their business-and I will go through the motions, but it isn't the same. I will never feel the same again. I have come to terms with that finally. There is no way to go back in time and feel the feelings I enjoyed before 8:10 p.m. on Feb.10, 2011 because you were alive then.

It is amazing how someone can change your life forever with words, isn't it? How the words spoken by a doctor can allow you to take the next breath that will give you peace or hell for the rest of your life. Or as long as you choose to live there.. Now, that I have vented somewhat-I already feel better. That is the purpose of this blog. To create a safe place for me to vent and feel whatever I need to feel in order to move forward and begin to heal from this tragic loss. I see a therapist and I PRAY daily...

You are welcome to join me here to vent, to pray, to request prayer or to share. Sometimes, reading is enough, but if you feel the desire to write-feel free to use the comment section, I do respond and I will join you in prayer requests. God listens in every language and He heals every heart. Sometimes, getting stuck like I did when I went in search of new photos takes me to a place I am not always comfortable with; it's not always a happy place. I guess that is why 'grief' is a journey and not a party, but we don't have to take the journey alone. As long as we keep moving forward, our journey continues, and the healing goes on..

Even in the midst of anger and frustration, God hears my need for release. His love is forever and always patient and I will continue to praise Him...because I know the power of prayer and faith as a mother grieves.

Saturday, July 28, 2012

I'm Predicting Rain Today

There is a good chance of rain today-you probably won't see that on the weather channel or hear it on the radio though...I don't care what the weatherman says-I am predicting rain today. The clouds are not puffy and white and the sky is not all blue, the breeze has the feel to it. The air has that scent in it...it is rain. The Farmer's Almanac may not show it-the stars might not align and the moon might not be in the right position, but I bet it rains today.

If I was a betting person-I would put money on it-today is the day-turn off your sprinklers... I do not have arthritis, I have heartritis...my joints don't get sore, my heart hurts... There is no sale on weather vanes. I just think it might rain... Why? I always heard when Angels are weeping. It is raining; it's their tears being shared from Heaven...

And today is J-Bug's birthday. Shanny being Shanny will be saddened by the thought of missing this very special day with him. Holding him close and snuggling him.

So, if you feel a raindrop or two, it might just be the tears of an Angel Mom who is missing her little boy on his special day. Please say an extra prayer for J-Bug to enjoy his day and know and feel the love surrounding him today and every day from here and Heaven!

As for me, I will continue to pray, because I know the power of prayer and faith as a mother grieves.

Sunday, July 29, 2012

Changes

I have written so much about feelings over the past months. Feelings are largely my world at the moment. Filling up every bit of space is a 'feeling.' I often wondered was it the same before Shanny died. Did I 'feel' so intensely? I don't think so. But, this is my world for now. I am finding a way to live in it, survive in it, cope in it and love in it.

Everyone grieves differently-my daughters, you, me, Jason and the man next door. No two journeys are alike. They are our own and meant to be personal. I believe God accompanies each of us and gives us all opportunities to reach out to Him along the way. He gently takes our hand and our heart and cradles us until we are strong enough to face the world again. For some, it might mean months and maybe, years. Some of us will never fully recover or find our "normal" again. Sadly, some of us become comfortable in our grief and choose to live in the depth of sorrow and despair. We may turn to alcohol or drugs to drown out the pain, or dull it for a time; but in existing inside our grief, it does not allow us to breathe or heal.

My therapist is wonderful about explaining my feelings and reassuring me I am 'normal.' My mini-breakdowns in a store, my seeing young women that look like Shanny all over the place, the memories that bring back the terror of those last spoken words of the doctor, and all of the other incidents that I cope with daily are all part of this journey back from the loss of a loved one. It is a comfort for someone to assure me I am not losing my mind some days...

What I am noticing is that my relationship with people I once felt close to is changing. I no longer feel that sense of kinship pain unfolded within us. There was a time that allowed us to bond within our pain. Since moving outside some of that pain, our relationship is moving in a different direction. Do I like it? No. Can I control it? No. I can only pray that a new bond will replace the other one built on our new found strength and ability to cope and function within our world of grief as we know it. I must confess-

some of these changes are scary. Shanny was the glue that held together some relationships in my world. Without her in it, there doesn't seem to be much reason to pursue those relationships now. They were based pretty much on Shanny as the focal point. The common link is no more a part of my world. I have no interest in maintaining the relationship, and apparently-neither do they show interest. Does it hurt? Yes? Is it part of life? Yes. Sadness overwhelms me sometimes, when I look back on it, but it doesn't change the fact that the pain outweighs the memory...

And that seems to be how this is progressing. Many of the friends and relationships once cherished when Shannon was here seem to bring pain now that she isn't here. How can that be? What triggers that feeling? Is this something we all experience in our grief process?

What I do know is this-family is a constant in one's life. That does not change. My children and my grand-children bring me great joy and peace. I see and feel Shannon in them and through them and they comfort me. I hope someday, they will say the same of me after I am gone...that when they think of me, I made them smile.

Thank you, Shanny for teaching me so much about family values and the willingness to move past hurts and move forward in love and to cherish memories that built a loving and strong family. Thank you for showing me how faith can remove fear and how trust in the Lord can cure your biggest heart aches.

I will try to embrace change and not be afraid, and I will continue to pray because you taught me ...the power of prayer and faith in life and now, as a mother grieves.

Tuesday, July 31, 2012

Lord, I am Praying for a New Heart

One that is not broken, Lord

No, not for me...for all those that do not know You.

When my heart breaks, I know You will mend it...

Every act of love You show me gently heals

one more jagged edge.

Every time Your forgive a sin,

or reckless act of selfishness, gently rubs a softer edge.

Lord, You heal.

That is why my prayer is for a New Heart...

For all those that are yet unfamiliar with

Your loving touch and gentle hand...

The hearts of my family, too,

Lord...some are bruised and hurting, they need tending

and I know your massage will ease their pain.

Some of the little ones hearts are shattered,

Lord, they miss their momma so.

Only You have the power

to heal their hearts in the absence of their mother's love.

My prayer is that you ease their pain

with the memory of a happier time,

one where they could feel the love that only a mother can give.

Let them hold onto that love,

Father and carry it in their hearts forever.

There is a husband without a wife,

who weeps for the comfort that only she could bring...

I pray you fill his heart with comfort and you give him peace.

Lord. Let the treasured moments he carries

remind him of the love that created their beautiful family

as he walks his journey.

Sisters whose hearts are torn by past decisions,

let them move forward in Your forgiveness and love.

My heart is quick to anger, Lord.

When loved ones hurt and I cannot fix it,

I become anxious and frustrated.

Remind me to give it to You, Lord...

You are the Only One

who can truly heal our wounds and our hearts.

I am only another broken heart...

I will not cease praying because I know the power of prayer and

faith as a mother grieves.

Wednesday, August 1, 2012

I Hope You Can Come

Shanny,

Today your sister is getting capped...that's a term used in nursing. She has kept her promise to you (and herself) to finish school-she chose nursing school and she is doing great! It's not easy but it's worth it...

Anyway, today at 2:00 pm she will be presented with a nursing 'cap' by her Aunt Geri. Only another nurse can actually do the capping. Isn't that a wonderful honor? I so wish you were here to see her. She always looked up to you. I don't think she realized how much she admired you until you weren't here to go to, or ask questions, or even argue with sometimes..

We actually have study shifts with Lulu so she can study at night for tests. It is a family affair and we are all the better for it. Another lesson, you have managed to teach us, sweetie. You have always been the wise one. Sometimes, I thought you were too big for your britches, I know...a little too mouthy but now I

know you only meant to offer very sage advice, because you were

correct in a lot of what you had to say-the content was there, the

delivery might have been a little rough at times..

Kimmy will be there, of course. Those two still argue like

crazy, but let anyone else try and get in the middle of their

argument, watch out! They really are the epitome of sisterly

love...they both know that is all you wanted from them-was their

sisterly love and they regret the times they were too busy or not

willing to bend to meet you half way. But, sometimes Shanny, you

have to admit-you were a little hard on them. It doesn't matter now,

does it? We can't forgive and forget; we can only remember and

hold dear the many loving memories you shared with us.

It's 3:35 in the a.m.; some days I still don't sleep for missing

you, but it isn't as intensely painful as it was, I can cope better

now. I am familiar with this reality-knowing you are not going to be

here when I wake up, that I can't call you, hug you or kiss you...yes,

it hurts but acceptance is closer.

The power of prayer and faith generated that acceptance to date...I could not have made it this far on my own. I know that. People from all over, some I do not know are praying, God hears all of our prayers for each other, because I pray for other people in pain, too. I have to step outside myself in order to breathe in the new day. God gives us an opportunity every day to make the most of His world; I can't do that all wrapped up in only my grief. I have to strip it away as much as I can and breathe deeply of His blessings. Then, share what I have learned and come to know as His truth-His love never fails.

Anyway, just a reminder-today 2:00 pm, come be with us, we'll be expecting you... because I know the power of prayer and faith as a mother grieves.

Thursday, August 2, 2012

I Remember

Every day I think of you I remember your smile. I remember how you crinkled your nose and touched your lip sometimes with your index finger when you giggled about my lips...

I remember how you said, "Are you crazy?", after I said something you found extra silly...I remember how you used to call me to talk and you would carry on a conversation with the kids most of the time. You always said at least you got to hear my voice. That makes me smile now.

I remember how I used to dread wearing something I bought to show you, because you were pretty tough on me. I am better for it now, though. I am more careful as I dress. When I am shopping I often catch myself saying-that is so Shanny! I remember you snuggling on your couch with your blanket; I still touch it sometimes and feel for the satin edge.

I remember how you could wear your hair any way you chose and it pretty much looked good-that hasn't changed for me, I still struggle with my hair, but I smile when I think of you...

I remember your flowers and Spring planting and your yard-David and I are working on our yard. We have a little Shanny garden...I remember the shoes, lots and lots of shoes. David's not so happy about this one; I have lots and lots of shoes, too. - .enough said...I remember the garage sales-David keeps trying to get me to just give the stuff away or call someone to haul it away, but the tax deduction, I smile...I remember our 'short'

shopping, errands, and 6 hours later we'd get home, tired and

hungry and arms filled with necessary packages... right.

I remember the books we shared, I loved how we shared our

thoughts on them, how we might read the same book - but have

two different ideas. It was wonderful time spent with a wonderful

daughter. I remember eating food I had never tried before at your

house-and liking it! Grilled foods, cooked foods, raw foods,

asparagus, leeks, hummus...yum! I am so much healthier now. I

remember seeing you with your kids, snuggling and giggling and

loving them...wishing I had been a better mom. I remember seeing

you and Jas all dressed up for a Justice Ball when I was sitting,

and thinking-they are like magic, what a beautiful couple...You two

made marriage look wonderful!

I remember the struggles with each child and your

relationship and yet, you knew the outcome would be good-you

always said so. You had such great faith. I remember you did so

much in a day for so many, and you never talked about it...you

never made your day sound overloaded or crammed, you just did.

You loved life.

You have been one of the three greatest blessings in my life and the memories I hold dear and close to my heart. You live there now, nestled there, where I can hold you and hug you and remember because I know the power of prayer and faith as a mother grieves.

Friday, August 3, 2012

A New Day

I am trying to decide what that means to me? I have choices

to make in this life that have changed over the years significantly.

Including the choice I face today, to live in the moment instead of

prior to God calling you home.

True, when I live there I am engulfed in the memories of

your smile, your warmth and love and seeing you with your family-

where you belong, but then...

I miss out on seeing my family-here with me now. My eight

grand-blessings and my two beautiful daughters that amaze me

with the women they have become and the mothers they are

proving to be. You'd be so proud, Shanny. They really are

special...

I miss out on the moments I share with David-the quiet,

special moments of unspoken love and understanding he gives me

because he knows and he miss you, too. August 1st was his mom's birthday and he spoke of it, and we said how much we loved and missed her and he came back to this moment. He chose to look to today for all it holds rather than live in the yesterdays with the memories...

Some days, it seems that choice is easier. I wonder why? I know all the psycho-babble I see a therapist and I am working on the grief, but I think it is more heart than head...

I love you; Shanny and I miss you all the way to Heaven and back a thousand times a day, always know I carry you in my heart... I cannot bring your physical presence back, it's true but I can always have you close in my heart, you are just a thought and a memory away. I do not like when people I love become memories. It saddens me that I cannot express my love to them and not for them anymore...

And yet, I know God has a reason and a purpose and I know He never takes me to a place and just drops me off-He never leaves me alone-He is always with me to face my fears and my pain. His Holy Spirit comforts me in times of great stress and tribulation. He is, well, He just is...

And so, on this new day I will rise and greet the moment with a smile and promise to make the most of this day. I will do some random act of kindness in your honor and hope to pass it on along with a smile...

...because I know the power of prayer and faith as a mother grieves!

Saturday, August 11, 2012

I Took A Moment to Be Happy

I arrived home yesterday from vacationing at the beach.
The house was fine. Our Sierra was happy to see us, Harley
was hungry as usual, and clutter was as we left it in a hurry to get
away. But, there are things that will never change and I kind of like
that...I am getting comfortable in my age and I am beginning to
accept Shanny's new residence is Heaven forevermore. I still miss
her like crazy, just like I missed Kim and Tina and the Grand 8
when I was beaching it...but it is a softer pain some days...it is
getting more bearable.

When I was shelling, Shanny would gift me with feathers
along the way to remind me she was close by...sure, they might
have been bird feathers, but I prefer to think of them as Angel
feathers, it makes me smile. She played with me in the early
morning waves and we giggled at the sand between our toes...she

will be with us next year and the year after that as well, wherever we vacation..

My girls were in my thoughts a lot, too. I spoke to them several times. Kimmy worked a lot that week. Tina had several doctor appointments and kept me up to date. I will fill you in and ask for prayer that her medicine works though...I am not sure what Beta Blockers are but she is on them and needs them to work, so please pray with me for that to happen.

Also, my sister had a hip replacement that went well, while I was away. God hears prayers from everywhere-even on the beach! Isn't He an awesome God? Now, we pray for a smooth and less painful recovery...

The only thing I really tried to not think about was work...I did pray for the Veterans and my co-workers, as I always do, but I didn't worry about the work on my desk, until I just let it cross my mind...oh, well, it will be there Monday!

The water was wonderful, in spite of a few jellyfish stings, the skies were warm and sunny, except for a few clouds and downpours, the company was great and the memories were wonderful...coming home to family- priceless!

But I took a moment to be happy on my journey and to remember the laughter, the sunshine on my face and the warmth in my heart-God gave it to me for a reason-He wants me to remember, so I will pray and continue to pray...because I know the power of prayer and faith as a mother grieves!

Sunday, August 12, 2012

Back to Real

Today is Sunday. I will go to church and sit in the pew with J-Bug, Eva and Gus and remember Shanny. Oh, I will say my prayers and stand, and kneel and make the sign of the cross, but God knows my heart is full of longing for my daughter, especially on Sundays. It was the day I saw her most often.

When I take the kids to Children's Liturgy, I still close my eyes and picture her standing with the red Children's book and reading from the Liturgist sheets of the day. Then we would work on our project together with all the kids. I didn't realize it then, just how much it would come to mean to me...those memories are my "real."

How I loved our little chats on the phone. Mostly, it was Shanny calling and whispering...mom, I can't talk long, just called to say hi...or, I'm on my way back into the building but I had a second and thought I would call...and sometimes, she was picking the kids up and I would hear her talking with them most of the way, but she loved me enough to call...that is my "real."

She'd call me and say mom, I have a few little errands to run, want to go? Now, even on a slow day, Shanny could go for hours without blinking. Usually, it meant we would be gone for four or five hours, visit at least that many stores, stop for something to eat, and she would have marked off only about half her list! But, she was still smiling as Gus was sleeping soundly in his car seat, she would say, isn't he just the cutest little guy ever, mom? That's my "real."

I loved to babysit when Shanny and Jason went out somewhere dressy. I loved seeing them together. It always made my heart smile. Jason would be in a fancy suit or tux, and Shanny would be in a cocktail dress with just the right touch of jewelry, I sell jewelry and she wore some of my pieces and modeled them for me before they left for the evening. She would take your breath away, she was so naturally beautiful...that was my "real."

I remember when she would get her hair done. Shannon had the silkiest, most beautiful blond hair I have seen. But, she was a woman with her own mind and she wanted her hair a certain way...she would go and have it cut and colored to meet her standards, right? Well, when I saw her, it always looked like her own natural hair color, so I couldn't really tell the difference. She would get really upset with me if I didn't comment on her hair, so after a while, I caught on and would say every so often how nice her hair looked and asked her if she had just had it done...that was my "real."

If I could advise you of anything and I am not saying I can, but-if you are given the blessing of time with your children and grandchildren-get "real" with them. Make memories with them. You don't have to go fancy places or do anything special-being together, sharing time, that is what makes "special" meaningful. Give your child or grandchild a 'thing', and they are bound to lose it, break it, or pack it away; give them a memory and you have given them a priceless gift. We don't know God's plan for tomorrow, but we are here today, so let's make the most of it. I know I will, because this mom knows the power of prayer and faith as a mother grieves!

Wednesday, August 15, 2012

Unapologetically, Shanny

I never knew someone who was as comfortable in their own skin as my daughter. She had her own thoughts, beliefs and concerns. From what I know, she stuck to them, too. I am proud of that. She stood up for what she believed in-in today's world that is saying much.

When she was younger, she had normal misgivings...look, I'm getting a zit, to, is that a gray hair?!? But, for the most part, Shannon loved what God blessed her with-all 96 pounds of her! Well, maybe 102.

Shannon lived her life out loud. She spoke her mind. She shared her thoughts, her words and her heart. If she had it to give, she gave it. That included her time. She not only worked full-time, she sat on several committees, worked for the kids' school, was a children's liturgist and was becoming politically active in the neighborhood to make it a safer, greener better place. She was active in her job for recycling and going green, as well. My daughter loved life and the people in it. She rarely saw the bad in people and refused to speak badly about anyone, unless you hurt her family. Then, you were chopped liver!

Shannon grew her faith from that of a mustard seed. I know, because I planted the mustard seed. I was not very active in the church or faith. She actually brought me back to God through her sharing her faith with me! God has a plan and it is much greater than any we could ever have for ourselves. Through His plan, she taught me His love is endless and His mercy is forever. Somehow, she talked me into getting involved with Children's Liturgy at St. Luke's. At first, I remember trying to come up with excuses to avoid that Sunday. I just wasn't into it. Church, especially the Catholic Church, didn't answer many questions for me and I didn't have much to offer it. But between Shanny and God, my life was going to change a great deal over the next couple of years. It has been changing ever since and because of the seed Shannon planted, the foundation of faith took hold again.

Before long, I was actually looking forward to those Sundays. I began to realize how much I loved spending that time with my Grandchildren and how much I was getting to know each one of them a little better. I began to see how God was working in my life and how I was being blessed in many ways.

Today, I wouldn't trade my Sundays for anything. I love the time I spend with the kids and Jason and God. Getting to know each of them a little better each week, and deepen my understanding of my desire to know God and His will.

Shannon was so wise for being so young. She just knew how to love on so many levels. I hope she sees me trying to be a better Mee Maw and Mom. I hope she knows she had a lot to do with teaching me about faith and God's love. I hope she knows I pray for her every day. I hope she knows I smile because of her every day. I hope she knows I dream of seeing her again in Heaven one day and having a group hug with all three of my Angels! I hope she knows I am proud she was always unapologetically Shanny!

Dear God, I want to take a deep breath and say a prayer of sincere praise and thanks for my blessings-my girls, Tina, my baby, Kimmy, my middle sweet, and Shanny, my firstborn Angel. And for all my blessings, my sons-in-law, my grand eight, and my loving family and friends, and the friends I have yet to meet. My journey has not been made alone. You have held me up the whole time in Your loving arms and kept me safe. Thank You, Jesus for Your strength, Your gentleness, and Your forever promise of eternal life.

Thank You for my Blessings and My memories. I am grateful I have lived to be blessed and I am able to reflect on the memories and know my Angel is with You in her Heavenly home, because this momma knows the power of prayer and faith as a mother grieves.

Friday, August 17, 2012

Ten More Days

Ten days from today you came into my life for the very first moment at mid-afternoon on a hot, humid day. I was huge by that time, swollen and cranky and so ready for you to be born. I was miserable from the summer heat and wildly excited to have my first baby. Scared, and ecstatic all at the same time...I remember all the false alarms, the whole family coming to the hospital and waiting patiently, only to be told-to go home, you weren't to be born that day...but a few weeks later, it was all so very real.

Having just turned twenty one a few months earlier and wanting desperately to prove my maturity to my family, I gritted my teeth and said-no drugs, I want to have a natural childbirth. Several hours later, I changed my mind, but it was too late. By 3:20 in the afternoon I was tired and you were well on your way, but decided to take just a few more minutes to make your first dramatic entry-that should have been a sign to me. My life was about to change, forever.

At 3:27 you came into this world with a sweet little wail and reddish blond hair, all 8 pounds and 6 ounces of you. You were so welcomed by so many, tiny and beautiful, proclaimed all in good health by the doctors and ready to go home a few days later. I was terrified as a new mother, terrified of failing. I wasn't sure how to nurse you, change you, bathe you, feed you, or "swaddle" you. Hence, the march of the Grandmothers began.

First, Great-grandmother Tillie, then Grandma Rosenthal, then Mi-Mi, all were marvelous when I look back, so loving and knowledgeable, kind and concerned for both you and me. They all knew that being a new mom meant a lot of sleepless nights and busy days. What I didn't know about was a little thing called post-par tum blues. I had gained a lot of weight, about 76 pounds, and I was depressed and guilt-ridden. I wanted my size 2 body, not this size 14 post-delivery, when are you due body.

I joined a gym and eight weeks later, I was a nursing, fat-free, yogurt-eating mother on a serious diet. But I was healthy and happy and on my way to smiling again. I could now feed you, burp you, bathe you, change you, and dress you without the fear of breaking a limb. All was good in the world of my newborn! Friends and family came to visit and raved about your beauty. You were a very sweet, content baby, who loved to play and smile and had a favorite blankie, thanks to your Mi-Mi. You were my first little Angel that God blessed me with, and I was overjoyed.

In ten days, I will celebrate that day, your birth into this world. There is also sadness about that day now. For it is no longer a day we can celebrate together. Your home is now in Heaven, with Your Heavenly Father. It is a beautiful memory, though, a blessing from above, just like you...And I will always cherish that day, the way I cherish you. I will keep it dear and near to my heart, where I keep you, as I thank God for my blessings, because this mother knows the power of prayer and faith as a mother grieves!

Afterword

I remember in the beginning, it was hard to feel. I walked around hollow and somewhat brittle. I heard people speaking and I am sure I responded to them, but I don't think it always came from my heart. Probably, my head spoke and the words came out of my mouth, and that was it. My bones felt hollow. I had no energy and I had no desire to regain my former self because I knew my world would never be the same.

There was rushing sounds some days. Like water rushing over rocks and down gullies, fast and faster it would gush, that was my mind numbing itself against the pain. I fought to keep my eyes closed because reality would seep in the second I opened them. In sleep there was a chance it was only a bad dream. I must admit, being awake was little different than being asleep, pain was so overwhelming-there was room for little else. My mind, body and it felt as if even my soul were being consumed by this horrific unstoppable, life-eating pain. I barely functioned in the beginning. I went from the bed to the bathroom and back to bed for the first three or four weeks.

I attempted to go out once to take my dog to the groomer, who is only five minutes away. I got lost and sat in the car and cried for half an hour sobbing. I finally took her into the groomer and when they noticed my tear-streaked face and asked if I was okay, I blurted out my daughter died a few weeks ago and I got lost and I am lost and I apologized for being late. They were kind but really didn't know what to say and thank goodness another customer came into the shop, so I left.

That's pretty much how the first months of grief were for me. Clouded moments of clarity doused with intense pain and reality, followed by restless sleep and gulping sobs of breathless ranting, silently raving in my head some days, wanting answers that would not come. I was praying for a miracle that could not come. And I was coming to terms with a world that no longer had my beloved daughter in it.

My faith won out. God allowed me anger and frustration and sadness, but He never allowed me the feeling of total hopelessness. Never did I experience, such desperation that I felt separated from God. I knew He was there, patiently waiting, allowing me to experience emotions that only my heart could speak of later. He did not rush me through my valleys. He accompanied me, silently.

I have no doubt that it was the prayers of family and friends that raised me up through it all. Some days, most days, really-I had forgotten how to pray. God never once forgot my name. My guardian Angel watched over me night and day, and when I was ready, I began to pray again. Sometimes, just one word was all I could manage. One word is all it takes for God to listen. Sometimes, He listens to our silence. He loves us always whether we are quiet or loud, angry or not. He understands our pain and waits patiently for us to turn to Him. He weeps with us and for us, and gathers us up and in that precious moment we begin to feel a new heartbeat of life

It was the summer of 2011 and I was cold. My heart was still frozen and I function outside myself but hold onto the pain. I went to work and surrounded myself with pictures and silent 'hugs' from Heaven to get me through the days.

Gently, I was thawing~ God allowed the layers to slowly melt away and feeling to return. There is still pain, but there are also moments of pleasure now. I can feel love as I look at her pictures and even smile with her some days.

My grandchildren continue to nurture me with their antics. I am learning to let their love warm me and cherish the time I am allowed to be with them. Every moment counts in this world. Each child has a gift and is a gift to me. My Grand Eight!

In the warm months of 2012 there are days now, that I know and feel Shannon is safe and happy in the Arms of Our Heavenly Father. I never doubt that, I just don't always embrace it. I am coming to terms with it, and for now that is enough.

Moving in the right direction to me means reaching past my pain to help someone else with theirs. There are now days I hug someone else who needs comfort. Now, I speak words of consolation and hope, and most days I actually believe them.

I do not put expectations on myself. I pray for guidance and strength. I pray for knowledge of God's will for me, and I pray for clarity of purpose. I ask God every day, to allow my faith to be child-like and true. I want to help others, but I know I cannot help others until I am whole and healed.

I choose happy today~ it's a start!

In Loving Memory
of
"Shanny"
Shannon Dodson
8-27-1976
to
2-10-2011

Made in the USA
San Bernardino, CA
27 March 2014